Step-by-step guide to Google Apps Script Book 4 – Documents

by

Barrie "Baz" Roberts

Learn

Google Workspace

& Apps Script

Table of Contents

Introduction

In this book we're going to work through a number of different real-life projects, where you'll see how we can use Google Apps Script in connection with the Google Docs to create a whole range of documents.

The chapters build on each other, and we start off with a simple master document copier and finish with connecting to Wikipedia and extracting data for a rugby tournament, then emailing someone the data in a formatted document.

As this is the fourth book in a series on Google Apps Script, I wanted to push readers, like yourself, into creating more sophisticated code, whilst giving you real-world examples, which you can either adapt for your own life or to inspire you to create some great code.

This book does assume you know the basics of Google Apps Script, JavaScript, HTML, and a little CSS. It also builds on the knowledge in my previous books, but as always I will be taking you, step-by-step through each project, to guide you through the code, to make sure you can understand what I've written and why I've done so, in order you can use it in your own projects.

At the back of the book, you'll find links to the complete codes in each chapter, plus a link to a folder containing a copy of the files used in this book.

So, as this book is based around Google Docs, let's start off by looking at the **Document Service** and how it's structured.

Document Service Overview

Before starting to work with the Document Service, we need to have an overall idea as to how it's structured. For the most part, it's pretty logical as it unsurprisingly follows the structure of how a Google Doc is put together. Here's a summary of the document layout and how the different parts fit together.

In a document, there are 4 main areas: Body, HeaderSection, FooterSection, and FootNote

Document
    ↪ **Body**
        ↪ ListItem
        ↪ Paragraph
        ↪ Table
        ↪ Table of Contents
    ↪ **HeaderSection**
        ↪ ListItem
        ↪ Paragraph
        ↪ Table

- ↳ **FooterSection**
    - ↳ ListItem
    - ↳ Paragraph
    - ↳ Table
- ↳ **Footnote**
    - ↳ ListItem
    - ↳ Paragraph

As you can see, there are different levels to the document and to access a lower level you need to access the higher ones first. For example, to add a paragraph to the body, you first need to access the document, then the body, then the paragraph.

You can also see that some things are not possible, for example, to add a table of contents to the header, or a table to the footnote.

Let's now look at the next level down.

This is adapted from this web page which details the structure of a document: https://developers.google.com/apps-script/guides/docs

Body
- ↳ **ListItem**
    - ↳ Equation
    - ↳ Footnote
    - ↳ HorizontalRule
    - ↳ InlineDrawing
    - ↳ InlineImage
    - ↳ PageBreak
    - ↳ Text
- ↳ **Paragraph**
    - ↳ Equation
    - ↳ Footnote
    - ↳ HorizontalRule
    - ↳ InlineDrawing
    - ↳ InlineImage
    - ↳ PageBreak
    - ↳ Text
- ↳ **Table**
    - ↳ TableRow
        - ↳ TableCell
            - ↳ Paragraph...
            - ↳ ListItem...
            - ↳ Table...

↳ **TableOfContents**
    ↳ Paragraph...
    ↳ ListItem...
    ↳ Table...

HeaderSection
  ↳ **ListItem**
    ↳ HorizontalRule
    ↳ InlineDrawing
    ↳ InlineImage
    ↳ Text
    ↳ UnsupportedElement (page number, etc.)
  ↳ **Paragraph**
    ↳ HorizontalRule
    ↳ InlineDrawing
    ↳ InlineImage
    ↳ Text
    ↳ UnsupportedElement (page number, etc.)
  ↳ **Table**
    ↳ TableRow
      ↳ TableCell
        ↳ Paragraph...
        ↳ ListItem...
        ↳ Table...

FooterSection
  ↳ **ListItem**
    ↳ HorizontalRule
    ↳ InlineDrawing
    ↳ InlineImage
    ↳ Text
    ↳ UnsupportedElement (page number, etc.)
  ↳ **Paragraph**
    ↳ HorizontalRule
    ↳ InlineDrawing
    ↳ InlineImage
    ↳ Text
    ↳ UnsupportedElement (page number, etc.)
  ↳ **Table**
    ↳ TableRow
      ↳ TableCell
        ↳ Paragraph...
        ↳ ListItem...
        ↳ Table...

FootnoteSection
  ↳ **ListItem**
        ↳ HorizontalRule
        ↳ Text
  ↳ **Paragraph**
        ↳ HorizontalRule
        ↳ Text

The header and footer options are similar to the body except that some options aren't available. As you can see from above, the main items that can be added and edited are lists, paragraphs, and tables. Within them we have a horizontal rule, drawings and images, and text, along with a few other less common items.

I highly recommend you look at the Google documentation on the Document Service here: https://developers.google.com/apps-script/reference/document

This details all the classes, methods, and attributes available to you.

Let's get coding!

1: Creating a Google Doc from a form submission

In this chapter, we're going to create an assignment based on the selection made in a Google Form.

Overview

1) The user will fill in the form, with their name and group and select an assignment they want to make and then submit the form.
2) The script will then get that response.
3) It will get the assignment number that has been selected and get the corresponding task for it.
4) It will then create a Google Doc and add their name, group and the task to it. This will be stored in their My Drive.

The idea here is that there is a bank of master assignments and the teachers can make a copy of these, adding their details via the form.

Key learning points

1) How to get the responses from a form
2) How to select text based on that submission
3) How to create a new Google Doc
4) How to append the text as paragraphs to the new document

First, we'll need to set up the form.

Go to Drive, click New > Google Forms

I have assumed you know how to make a Google Form. If not, I highly recommend reading my book "Beginner's Guide to Google Forms" ;)

Form

1-Assignment Maker

Form to make an assignment master for a particular teacher and group

Teacher *

1. Paul Mac

2. George Harris

3. Jo Lennon

4. Ringo Estar

Group *

1. A1

2. B1

3. B2

Which assignment do you want to make? *

◯ Assignment #1

◯ Assignment #2

◯ Assignment #3

The first question is the teacher's name, the second, their group, and finally the assignment they want to make.

In this script, we're going to bind the script to the form. Click on the 3-dot menu and select "Script editor".

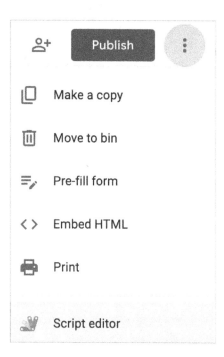

Let's name the file "Assignment Maker". Now let's get into the code.

The code

```
1.  //CHAPTER 1
2.  function assignmentMaker(e) {
3.    //Get latest form response (teacher, group, assignment)
4.    const itemResponses = e.response.getItemResponses();
5.    const teacher = itemResponses[0].getResponse();
6.    const group = itemResponses[1].getResponse();
7.    const assignment = itemResponses[2].getResponse();
```

Line2: Open the function and notice that we are passing event information, here labelled 'e'.

L4: We first need to get the latest item responses, which are stored in the event. We get these from the event response and it returns an array of item responses.

L5-7: Then we need to get the specific responses within that. In this case, we need to get the 3 separate responses, the teacher's name, their group, and the assignment and store them in separate variables. Note, the array positions, 0, 1, 2.

```
9.        //Get task for assignment selected
10.       const assignments = ["Assignment #1",
11.       "Assignment #2",
12.       "Assignment #3"];
13.
14.       const tasks = ["Write about your last holiday.",
15.       "Write a review of a film you watched recently.",
16.       "Write a proposal for a new shop in your town."];
```

L10-12: Here, we've got the 3 possible assignments stored in an array.

L14-16: Here, we've got the tasks that correspond with those assignments. The important thing here is that they are in the same order as the assignments, as that's how we're going to be able to get the correct task.

```
18.       const position = assignments.indexOf(assignment);
19.       const task = tasks[position];
```

L18: Now, let's get the position in the array of the assignment that was selected. We use **indexOf()** to find the position of it. This will return a number from 0 to 2.

L19: Now, let's get the task at that position. So, now we have the text stored in the *task* variable.

```
21.       //Create G Doc in My Drive, get body & append paragraphs
22.       const doc = DocumentApp.create(assignment);
23.       const body = doc.getBody();
24.       body.appendParagraph("Teacher: " + teacher);
25.       body.appendParagraph("Group: " + group);
26.       body.appendParagraph(task);
27.       }
```

L22: Let's create the new blank Google Doc. To do so, we use **DocumentApp** and the **create()** method. Let's use the assignment name as the name of the file, so we add that as a parameter.

The file will be created in your My Drive.

L23: Now, to add text to the main part of the document, we need to get its body, so we use the **getBody()** method on the document.

L24: To add the texts, here we're going to simply append them as paragraphs to the body, using **appendParagraph()**. The first one is "Teacher: " and the teacher's name.

L25-27: Then add the group name and finally, add the task. Close the function.

The trigger

All that is needed now is to add a trigger, so that the program runs automatically when someone submits a form.

Click on the clock icon on the left-hand side of the editor. Click "Add Trigger".

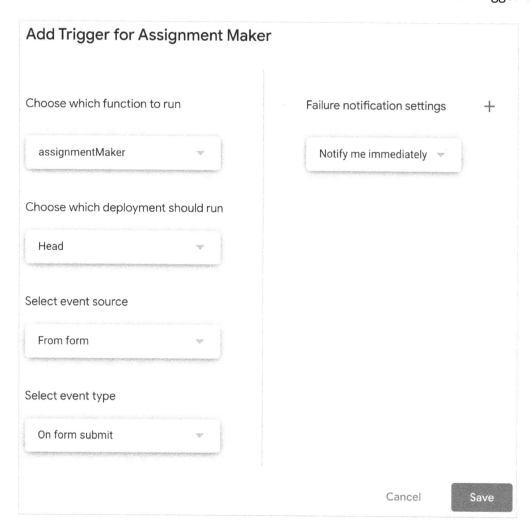

Change "Select event type" to "On form submit" and I usually want to get notified immediately if there are any errors, so the menu on the right I change to "Notify me immediately", but this will depend on your context. Click "Save".

Triggers

Owned by	Last run	Deployment	Event	Function
Me	Jun 26, 2023, 8:14:31PM	Head	From form - On form submit	assignmentMaker

Your trigger is now set up. Just close the window. Let's give it a go...

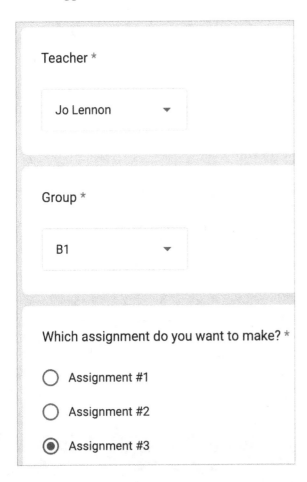

Teacher *

Jo Lennon ▼

Group *

B1 ▼

Which assignment do you want to make? *

◯ Assignment #1

◯ Assignment #2

◉ Assignment #3

We fill in the form and submit it.

Assignment #3

The doc is created in My Drive.

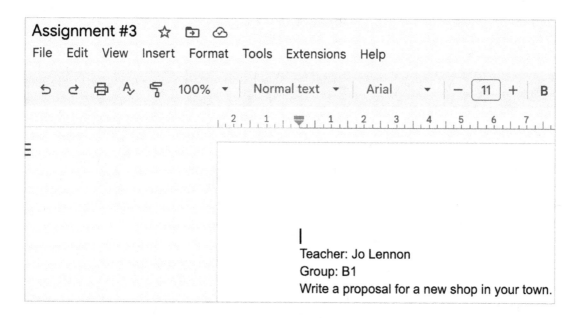

Opening the document, we can see it's added the text we want.

OK, this is quite a limited example, but we can see how easy it is to connect Google Forms with Google Docs.

2: Master document copier

In this chapter, we're going to allow teachers to use a Google Form to create a copy of a choice of two master documents, selected from a list, and to add it to a specific folder of ours.

Overview

1) The teacher will fill in the form and select the master document they want to make a copy of (either a lesson plan or class notes) and then submit the form.
2) The script will then get that response, get the appropriate document and folder.
3) It will make a copy of the document and get its body and paragraphs.
4) It will add different text, depending on the document selected.
   a. For the lesson plan, it will add the teacher's name near the top.
   b. For the class notes, it will add "Prepared by " plus the teacher's name at the bottom.

Key learning points

1) How to copy a master document.
2) How to get a document by its ID.
3) How to get all the paragraphs in a document.
4) How to append text to a specific paragraph.
5) How to insert a paragraph and text at the end of a document.

Form

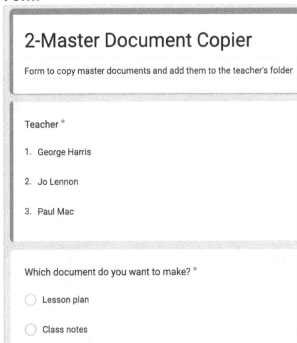

There are two fields, the teachers' names and the list of documents they can make.

Documents

 2-Class Notes MASTER

2-Lesson plan MASTER

We have two master Google Docs on our Drive.

NAME OF THE LESSON

Lesson Plan for Grade 7, Social Science

OVERVIEW & PURPOSE

Lorem ipsum dolor sit amet, consectetuer adipiscing elit, sed diam nonummy nibh euismod tincidunt ut laoreet dolore magna aliquam erat volutpat.

EDUCATION STANDARDS

1. Lorem ipsum dolor sit amet, consectetuer adipiscing elit.
2. Sed mollis aliquam nibh.
3. Pellentesque pellentesque dictum urna.

The lesson plan, which is one of Google Doc templates, will be edited so that the teacher's name will be added near the top.

COURSE NAME
FALL SEMESTER 20XX

no_reply@example.com

04 September 20XX

Lorem ipsum dolor sit amet, consectetuer adipiscing elit, sed diam nonummy nibh euismod tincidunt ut laoreet dolore magna aliquam erat volutpat.

Ut wisi enim ad minim veniam, quis nostrud exerci tation ullamcorper suscipit lobortis nisl ut aliquip ex ea commodo consequat.

- At vero eos et accusam et justo duo dolores et ea rebum
  - Ut wisi enim ad minim veniam.
  - Quis nostrud exerci tation ullamcorper.
  - Suscipit lobortis nisl ut aliquip ex ea commodo consequat.

Duis autem vel eum iriure dolor in hendrerit in vulputate velit esse molestie consequat, vel illum dolore eu feugiat nulla facilisis at vero eros et accumsan.

Lorem ipsum dolor

- At vero eos et accusam et justo duo dolores et ea rebum
  - Ut wisi enim ad minim veniam.
  - Quis nostrud exerci tation ullamcorper.

The course notes, also a Google Doc template, will be edited so that the teacher who has prepared it appears at the bottom.

So, let's look at the code.

The code

This script project is bound to the Google Form.

```
1. //CHAPTER 2
2. function copyMasterDocument(e) {
3.
4.   //Get form responses (teacher & document)
5.   const itemResponses = e.response.getItemResponses();
6.   const teacher = itemResponses[0].getResponse();
7.   const document = itemResponses[1].getResponse();
```

L2: Open the function and get the form event "**e**".

L5: First, we get the item responses in the response.

L6-7: Then within that response we have the teacher's name and the document they have selected. We get those by getting the 2 items in the *itemResponses* array.

```
9.       //Get file ID for document selected
10.      const documents = ["Lesson plan", "Class notes"];
11.      const documentIds = ["DOCUMENTID1",
12.                           "DOCUMENTID2"];
```

L10: In the array *documents*, we have the two document names.

L11-12: In the *documentIds* array, we have the IDs of those documents. Replace DOCUMENT1ID and DOCUMENT2ID with your own document IDs.

Now, we want to get the ID of the document selected.

```
14.      const docIndex = documents.indexOf(document);
15.      const docId = documentIds[docIndex];
```

L14: First, we get the index of the document name in the documents array, using **indexOf()**.

L15: Then we get the document ID using the position index we just got.

```
17.      //Get teacher's folder ID from teacher
```

```
18.        const teachers = ["George Harris", "Jo Lennon", "Paul Mac"];
19.
20.        const folderIds = ["FOLDERID1",
21.                           "FOLDERID2",
22.                           "FOLDERID3"];
```

L18: In the array *teachers*, we have the names of the teachers.

L20-22: In the array, *folderIds*, we have the IDs of the teacher's folders, which we'll use to add the document into. Replace FOLDER1ID, etc with your own folder IDs.

```
24.        const teacherIndex = teachers.indexOf(teacher);
25.        const folderId = folderIds[teacherIndex];
```

L24-25: Similar to before, we first get the position of the teacher's name in the array using **indexOf()**. Then we use that position to get the folder ID for that teacher.

In this example, we're not going to create a new document like we did in the previous chapter, instead we're going to make a copy of a master document.

```
27.        //Get master Doc and make a copy and rename
28.        const doc = DriveApp.getFileById(docId);
29.        const tFolder = DriveApp.getFolderById(folderId);
30.        const copiedDoc = doc.makeCopy(document + " - " + teacher, tFolder);
```

L28: First, we get the master document by its ID, using **DriveApp**.

L29: Next, we get the teacher's folder by its ID.

L30: Then, we make a copy of the master document. In the brackets we give it the name we want. Here, I've passed the name of the document and the teacher's name. We also need to state which folder it's going to be created in, using the *tFolder* variable. We store the new document in a variable to be able to work with it.

```
32.        //Edit new Document - Add teacher's name to Doc
33.        const newDoc = DocumentApp.openById(copiedDoc.getId());
34.        const body = newDoc.getBody();
35.        const paragraphs = body.getParagraphs();
```

L33: To be able to access the body, etc of the document, we need to first open it by its ID. So, here we get the ID of the copied doc and then open it and store that opened document in the variable *newDoc*.

L34: We then get the document body.

L35: As we want to work with specific paragraphs, we first need to get all the paragraphs in the body, using **getParagraphs()**.

```
37.        //Append text to 3rd paragraph
38.        if (document === "Lesson plan") {
39.          paragraphs[2].appendText("Teacher: " + teacher);
40.        }
```

If the document is a lesson plan, we're going to add "Teacher: " and the teacher's name.

L42: Here, we use an **if** statement to check if the document is called "Lesson plan".

L43: Then, we get the 3rd paragraph (index: 2) and add the text using **appendText()**.

```
41.        //Insert paragraph at the end of the document
42.        else if (document === "Class notes") {
43.          body.insertParagraph(paragraphs.length, "Prepared by " + teacher);
44.        }
45.      }
```

L42: Alternatively, we check to see if the document is called "Class notes".

Note, we could just use an else statement here as a default, as it's either going to be a lesson plan or the other document.

L43-45: Here, we're going to insert a paragraph at the end. We could append as before, but let's use the **insertParagraph()** method to select where we're going to add it.

We want to get the last paragraph, so we can get that by getting the length of the *paragraphs* array. Then we add the text we want, in this case, "Prepared by " and the teacher's name.

Before using the form, we need to add a "On Form Submit" trigger, so that when the form is submitted, it runs the script, as we saw in chapter 1.

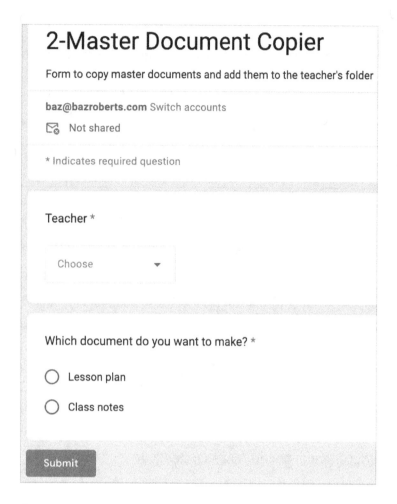

So, now the form is ready to be used. The teacher selects their name and chooses the document they want to make a copy of. They then submit the form.

Here's the lesson plan:

As we can see, it's added the document in their folder.

Plus, we can see it's added their name to the document.

Here are the class notes:

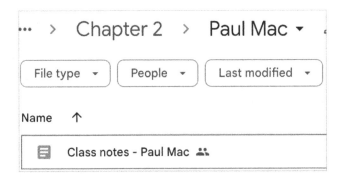

We can see it's added the document to their folder.

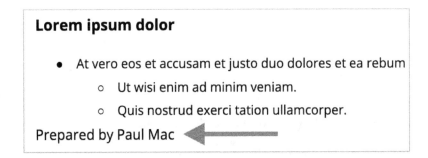

Plus, we can see it's added who has prepared it at the bottom.

Obviously, you can add far more text to these documents, but you can see it's easy to personalise them, while the manager can control the versions of the documents they are copying via the form.

3: Edit a document template using placeholders -Sales Quote

In this chapter, we're going to create a sales quote document from information stored in a Sheet.

Overview

1) The script will get all the values from the Google Sheet and remove the first 2 rows.
2) Then it will loop through the data and run only for rows where the checkbox has been ticked.
3) It will then format some of the data so it's ready to add to the document.
4) It will then make a copy of the Google Doc template and get its header and body.
5) Then it will replace the placeholders in the header with the company details from the sheet and then do the same for the placeholders in the body.
6) It'll add a link to another Google Doc (the terms and conditions).
7) It will add a link to the sales quote back on the sheet and then reset the checkboxes.

Key learning points

1) How to get data from a Google Sheet and loop through selected ones.
2) How to format that data so it appears correctly in our document.
3) How to edit the header as well as the body of the document.
4) How to replace placeholders in the template using replaceText().
5) How to add links to a document.
6) And finally, how to add a link to the document back in our sheet.

First, let's look at the sheet and the data we'll be entering and using.

Sheet

	A	B	C	D	E	F	G
1	**SALES QUOTES**						
2	Quote Number	Company Name	Company Address 1	Company Address 2	Customer Name	Customer address 1	Customer address 2
3	0001	Widgets Ltd	1, Big factory street	Big Town, 12345	Gizmos PLC	5, Grey Avenue	Smallish Town, 54321
4	0002	Chisme SA	10, Industrial park	Huge Town, 55555	Thingames PLC	3, Long Road	Pretty Place, 13579
5							

We have the quote number, the company details (as possibly different companies supply the products), and the customer's details.

H	I	J	K	L	M	N	O	P	Q
Prepared date	Expiry date	Delivery days	T&C Doc link	Item	Qty	Unit Price	Total	Quote Link	Make?
20/01/2023	28/02/2023	5	https://docs	Widgetoo	100	$2.00	$200.00	Link	☐
21/01/2023	31/03/2023	2	https://docs	Whatsit	50	$8.00	$400.00		☐
									☐

We also have the quote prepared and expiry dates, delivery days, and the link to the terms and conditions. Plus, we have the item requested, the quantity, unit price and the total. Finally, we have a column where the link to the quote will go and checkboxes which will tell the script which quotes to make.

Template

I'm using one of the Google Doc templates. Note, the placeholders we're going to replace are in the curly brackets in the template.

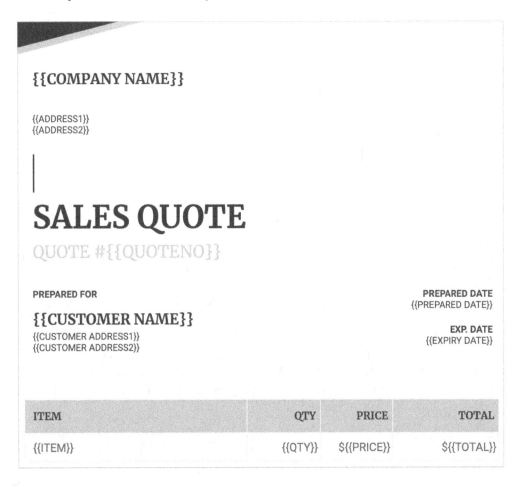

THIS QUOTATION IS SUBJECT TO THE FOLLOWING TERMS AND CONDITIONS:

1. Delivery will be made within {{DELIVERY DAYS}} days following {{CUSTOMER NAME}} receipt of payment.

2. The general terms and conditions of purchase apply to this quotation contract. See link below.

3. This quotation may be accepted to form a binding contract upon any one of the following options:

   a. Signature below and payment to {{COMPANY NAME}} for the items listed in this quote prior to the expiration date.

   b. Issuance of a purchase order to {{COMPANY NAME}} referencing this quote and the terms and conditions herein prior to the expiration date above.

{{TandC}}

There will be a link to this document too.

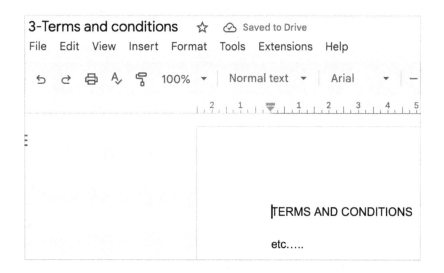

Let's look at the code.

As we're going to be working with a Google Sheet and then making the sales quotes from there, we're going to add the script project to the Sheet. So, first open the script editor in the Google Sheet found under the Tools menu.

The code

First, we'll need to get the sheet and its data, the master template, and the folder we want to add the sales quote into, and for later use, the time zone, so we can format the dates.

```
1. function makeSalesQuotes() {
2.    //Get quote data, master, folder & timezone
3.    const ss = SpreadsheetApp.getActiveSpreadsheet();
4.    const sh = ss.getSheetByName('QUOTES');
5.    const quoteMaster = DriveApp.getFileById('FILE ID');
6.    const fQuotes = DriveApp.getFolderById('FOLDER ID');
7.    const timeZone = Session.getScriptTimeZone();
8.    const data = sh.getDataRange().getValues();
9.    data.splice(0, 2);
```

L1: Open the function.

L3: Get the active spreadsheet.

L4: Then get the sheet called "QUOTES".

L5: Then get the quote master template by its ID. Add your document ID here.

L6: Get the folder where the sales quotes will be stored by its ID. Add your folder ID here.

L7: Get the time zone, which we'll use to format the prepared and expiry dates.

L8: Let's get all the data on that sheet. This allows us to just make one call. From now on we'll use the data in this array, which will speed up the program.

L9: We don't need the first 2 rows as they are the title and headers, so we can splice those out.

Now we're going to loop through that data and look for any rows of data that have the checkbox ticked.

```
11.    //Loop through quotes and make those ticked
12.    data.forEach((row, r) => {
13.      if (row[16] === true) {
```

L12: We use **forEach()** to loop through the data. Each row of data is stored in the variable *row* and each loop is counted and stored in the variable *r*, which we'll use to add information back to the right row on the sheet. Note, we're using new(ish) JavaScript arrow functions (=>) here.

L13: We add a check to see if column Q has been ticked. We do this by checking if the value in *row* in position 16 is equal to true, i.e. ticked. If so, it will run the code below, if not it will move on to the next row.

```
15.      //Set up variables for quote data
16.      const quoteNumb = row[0], compName = row[1], compAdd1 = row[2],
```

```
17.         compAdd2 = row[3], custName = row[4], custAdd1 = row[5],
18.         custAdd2 = row[6], preparedDate = row[7], expiryDate = row[8],
19.         delivery = row[9], tcLink = row[10], item = row[11],
20.         qty = row[12], price = row[13], total = row[14];
```

L16-20: Here, we'll store each piece of data as a variable with a name that identifies it easily.

The format on the sheet isn't automatically copied to the document, so here we'll need to format the data as we want to see it on the document.

```
22.         //Format data
23.         const quoteNo = ('0000' + quoteNumber).slice(-4);
24.         const price2 = price.toFixed(2);
25.         const total2 = total.toFixed(2);
26.         const prepared = Utilities.formatDate(preparedDate, timeZone, 'dd-MM-
    yyyy');
27.         const expiry = Utilities.formatDate(expiryDate, timeZone, 'dd-MM-
    yyyy');
```

L23: Getting the value "0001" from the sheet, will be stored as "1.0" in the script, so we need to format it back to a 4-digit number. To do this, we add 4 zeros to the number and then use **slice(-4)** to remove any additional digits, so it always ends up being a 4-digit number regardless of the number.

L24-25: Add 2 decimal points to the prices and totals, by using **toFixed(2)**.

L26-27: Here, we need to format the dates from the sheet.

Now, we have all the data we need, it's time to create the document.

```
29.         //Create quote document and get header and body
30.         const newQuote = quoteMaster.makeCopy("Quote #" + quoteNo, fQuotes);
31.         const newQuoteDoc = DocumentApp.openById(newQuote.getId());
32.         const header = newQuoteDoc.getHeader();
33.         const body = newQuoteDoc.getBody();
```

L30: First, we make a copy of the master template and store it in the folder we want. Here, I'm naming it "Quote # + the quote number".

L31: To work with it, we then need to open it by its ID.

L32-33: We're going to edit both the header and the body, so we need to get those.

Our template contains a number of placeholders in the format of {{TEXT}}. This is what we'll use to add the data from the sheet.

```
35.        //Replace placeholders in header
36.        header.replaceText('{{COMPANY NAME}}', compName);
37.        header.replaceText('{{ADDRESS1}}', compAdd1);
38.        header.replaceText('{{ADDRESS2}}', compAdd2);
```

L36-38: First, let's replace the placeholders in the header with the company name and address. To do this, we use the **replaceText(text to be replaced, new text)**. We use the variables we set up early for the new text.

Now, we do the same for the body. Here, we have lots of placeholders, so rather than write a **replaceText()** line for each one, we can store all the placeholders in an array, store all the new text variables in another, then loop through the placeholders and replace them.

```
40.        //Replace placeholders in body
41.        const placeholders = ['{{QUOTENO}}', '{{CUSTOMER NAME}}',
42.        '{{CUSTOMER ADDRESS1}}', '{{CUSTOMER ADDRESS2}}',
43.        '{{PREPARED DATE}}', '{{EXPIRY DATE}}',
44.        '{{ITEM}}', '{{QTY}}', '{{PRICE}}', '{{TOTAL}}',
45.        '{{DELIVERY DAYS}}', '{{COMPANY NAME}}'];
```

L41-45: Here, we store the placeholders. Note, they are all strings.

```
47.        const quoteData = [quoteNo, custName, custAdd1, custAdd2,
48.          prepared, expiry, item, qty, price2, total2, delivery,
49.          compName];
```

L47-49: Here, we store the list of variables that will replace the placeholders. It's essential that these variables are <u>in the same order</u> as the placeholders in the previous array.

Now, we loop through the placeholders replacing them with the new text.

```
51.        placeholders.forEach((ph, p) => {
52.          body.replaceText(ph, quoteData[p]);
53.        });
```

L51: We use the *placeholders* array and each placeholder is represented by the *ph*. The parameter *p* is keeping count as we loop through.

L52: As before, use **replaceText()** to replace the placeholders. We pass the placeholder *ph* and then get the new text from the *quoteData* array at position *p*.

The last thing we want to do in this document is to add a link to the term and conditions document.

```
55.        //Add link
56.        const link = newQuoteDoc.getBody().findText("{{TandC}}")
57.                          .getElement().asText();
58.        link.setLinkUrl(tcLink);
59.        body.replaceText("{{TandC}}", "Terms and conditions document");
60.        newQuoteDoc.saveAndClose();
```

L56-57: In the template, the link will be added where the placeholder "{{TandC}}" is located. First, we get the body and then using the **findText()** method, we find the text we want. To be able to edit it, we need to get the element and then get it as text. We store that in a variable.

L58: Then add the link URL we want to that variable, using **setLinkUrl(link)**.

L59: We've added the link but we also need to update the text. So, as we saw earlier, we use **replaceText()** to add the new text.

L60: Now, we've finished editing the document, we save and close it.

The final thing we want to do is to add a link to the new document back on the sheet and also to reset the checkbox.

```
62.        //Add quote link to sheet and reset checkbox
63.        const rowNo = r + 3;
64.        sh.getRange(rowNo, 16)
65.          .setFormula('=HYPERLINK("' + newQuote.getUrl() + '","Link")');
66.        sh.getRange(rowNo, 17).setValue("FALSE");
67.        }
68.      });
69.    }
```

L63: We will need the current row number on the sheet and we get that by adding 3 to the variable r. I've added it to a variable as we're going to use it twice below.

L64-65: Then set a hyperlink formula which uses the URL from the new file and displays the text "Link" on the sheet.

L66: We get the same row and this time the "Make?" column and set the checkbox to FALSE, which will untick the checkbox.

L67-69: We close the **if** statement, the **forEach** loop and the function.

Rather than run the code from the script editor, let's also add a menu to our sheet, so the script can be run from there.

OnOpen menu code

To add another script file, in the script editor click on the plus sign next to Files and select Script. I usually rename it 'menu' or 'onOpen'.

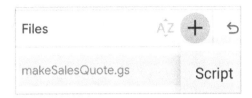

```
1. function onOpen() {
2.    const ui = SpreadsheetApp.getUi();
3.    ui.createMenu("QUOTE")
4.       .addItem("Make sales quotes", 'makeSalesQuotes')
5.       .addToUi();
6. }
```

L1: Set up the **onOpen()** function.

L2: Get the spreadsheet UI.

L3: Create the menu using **createMenu(Name)**.

L4: Add the menu item, using **addItem(Display name, function name)**.

L5-6: Then add it to the UI and close the function.

So, when the sheet is opened, the **onOpen()** function will automatically be triggered and the menu added.

OK, let's look at an example. Here I've added a quote, numbered 0002.

SALES QUOTES

Quote Number	Company Name	Company Address 1	Company Address 2	Customer Name	Customer address 1	Customer address 2
0001	Widgets Ltd	1, Big factory street	Big Town, 12345	Gizmos PLC	5, Grey Avenue	Smallish Town, 54321
0002	Chisme SA	10, Industrial park	Huge Town, 55555	Thingames PLC	3, Long Road	Pretty Place, 13579

Prepared date	Expiry date	Delivery days	T&C Doc link	Item	Qty	Unit Price	Total	Quote Link	Make?
20/01/2020	29/02/2020	5	https://docs	Widgetoo	100	$2.00	$200.00	Link	☐
21/01/2020	31/03/2020	2	https://docs	Whatsit	50	$8.00	$400.00		☑

A row on the spreadsheet is filled out with the quote details and at the end, the "Make?" checkbox is ticked. Note, multiple quotes can be made at the same time.

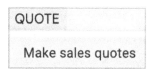

The user clicks the QUOTE menu and selects "Make sales quotes".

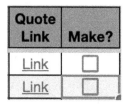

On the Sheet we can see it's added the link to the document and unticked the checkbox.

It has made the sales quote document and has stored it in the quote folder.

Opening the document, we can see it's added the information we wanted. The screenshots are in parts, so you can see the text a little better.

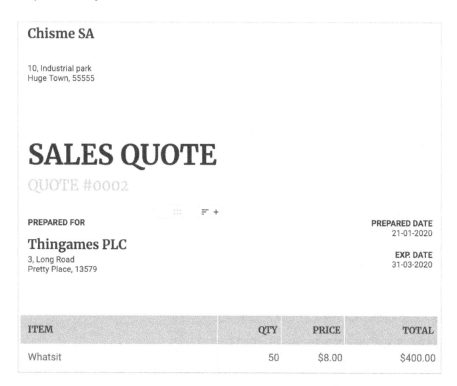

THIS QUOTATION IS SUBJECT TO THE FOLLOWING TERMS AND CONDITIONS:

1. Delivery will be made within 2 days following Thingames PLC receipt of payment.

2. The general terms and conditions of purchase apply to this quotation contract. See link below.

3. This quotation may be accepted to form a binding contract upon any one of the following options:

   a. Signature below and payment to Chisme SA for the items listed in this quote prior to the expiration date.

   b. Issuance of a purchase order to Chisme SA referencing this quote and the terms and conditions herein prior to the expiration date above.

Terms and conditions document

As you can see, it's really easy to get the information stored in a Google Sheet and add it to a Google Doc.

4: Making an invoice with multiple items -Invoice

In this chapter, we're going to dynamically create an invoice from information stored in a Google Sheet.

The limitation with the example in chapter 3 was that it only collected and added one set of data. Here, we're going to get various rows of data from a spreadsheet and display that in a table in a Google Doc.

Plus, as we used placeholders, we were limited to what we could add to the document. Here, we're going to create content based on what has been entered onto the sheet and this isn't limited to just one row of data.

Overview

1) The user selects an invoice number to make and runs the script from the menu.
2) The script will get all the values from the Google Sheet and remove the first 2 rows.
3) Then it will loop through the data and run only for rows which match the invoice number that has been selected.
4) It will then format some of the data so it's ready to add to the document, plus, get the data so that it's ready to be added as table rows.
5) It will then make a copy of the Google Doc template.
6) Then it will set up the format styles used in different parts of the document.
7) It'll edit the tables and add the data into them.
8) And finally, it works out the grand total of the items and adds that at the bottom of the second table.

Key learning points

1) How to use the **filter()** method to filter your data by a value.
2) How to use the **map()** method to return formatted rows of data from your sheet.
3) How to set up styles for documents, including font size, colours, alignment.
4) How to edit tables and add data to them. Plus, how to then format that data.
5) How to dynamically create a table based on data from the sheet.
6) And finally, how to use the **map()** and **reduce()** methods to calculate the total.

First, let's look at the sheet and the data we'll be entering and using.

Sheet

The company provides classes to companies and they are charged at an hourly rate.

	A	B	C	D	E	F	G
1	**INVOICES**				Invoice to make:		**0001** ⌄
2	**Invoice number**	**Company**	**Date**	**Classes**	**Hourly rate**	**Hours**	**Sub total**
3	0001	Widgets Ltd	18/01/2023	Class 01	$20.00	5	$100.00
4	0001	Widgets Ltd	18/01/2023	Class 02	$15.00	10	$150.00
5	0001	Widgets Ltd	18/01/2023	Class 03	$20.00	20	$400.00

Template

Here, we have two tables, the top part with the company name, date, and invoice number. The second table will detail the classes purchased, the number of hours, the hourly rate, the sub-totals and then the grand total at the bottom.

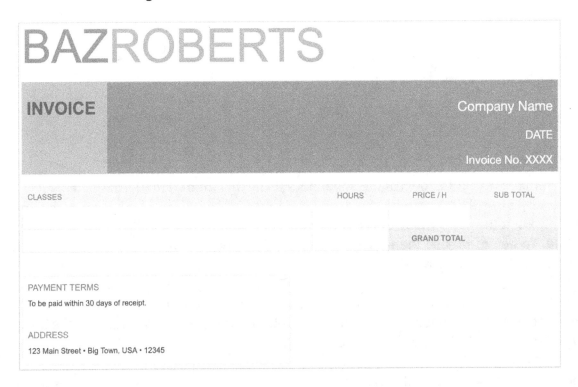

The code

This code is stored in the Script Editor of the Google Sheet, i.e. bound to the Sheet. First, we get the data from the spreadsheet, get our invoice template and the folder we want to add the invoices into.

```
1. function makeInvoice() {
2.   //Get invoice data
```

```
3.     const ss = SpreadsheetApp.getActiveSpreadsheet();
4.     const sh = ss.getSheetByName('INVOICES');
5.     const invoiceTemp = DriveApp.getFileById('FILE ID');
6.     const fInvoices = DriveApp.getFolderById('FOLDER ID');
7.     const timeZone = Session.getScriptTimeZone();
8.     const data = sh.getDataRange().getValues();
9.     const invoiceNum = data[0][6];
```

L1: Open the function.

L3-4: Get the active spreadsheet and the sheet called "INVOICES".

L5-6: Then get the invoice template and invoice folder by their IDs. Add yours here.

L7: Get the time zone to format the date later on.

L8: Then get all the data on the sheet.

L9: We get the invoice number that has been selected in cell G1.

```
11.        //Filter data by invoice selected
12.        data.splice(0, 2);
13.        const invoiceData = data.filter((row) => {
14.          return row[0] === invoiceNum;
15.        });
```

L12: We then remove the first 2 rows of the sheet data using the **splice()** method.

L13: As we only want the rows which correspond with the invoice number selected, we need to filter that data. To do so, we use the **filter()** method on the variable *data*. The parameter *row* is each row of data in the *data* array.

L14: We want to return the rows where the invoice number in column A matches the invoice number selected in cell G1. For each row, the cell in column A will be the first value in the array, so we get *row[0]* and check if it equals the invoice number.

The returned values are stored in the variable *invoiceData*. So, now we only have rows which match the invoice number.

```
17.        //Get company & date and format data
18.        const company = invoiceData[0][1], date1 = invoiceData[0][2];
19.        const invoiceNo = ('0000' + invoiceNum).slice(-4);
20.        const date = Utilities.formatDate(date1, timeZone,
21.         'd MMMMM yyyy');
```

L18: Get the company name and invoice date.

L19: I want the invoice number to be a 4-digit number, so we need to format the number, even though on the sheet it appears in that format already. As we saw in chapter 3, we add 4 zeros to it then slice the last 4 digits.

L20-21: We then format the date. Here, I want the format to be something like, "18 January 2023". Using the 5 Ms will display the month in full.

```
23.        //Get invoice info
24.        const invoiceRows = invoiceData.map((rw) => {
25.          return [rw[3], rw[5],
26.          "$" + rw[4].toFixed(2),
27.          "$" + rw[6].toFixed(2)];
28.        });
```

As we're going to be adding the details of the items purchased into a table and that there will be rows of data, we can grab the data from the sheet and store it in formatted rows, ready to add to our table later on.

L24: To do this, we will use the **map()** method, which will loop through the invoice data. Each row will be in the parameter *rw*.

L25-28: As we're going to return multiple items, we need to group it all together in an array. Then in the array we add the items we want. The beauty of this is that we can also format some of the data at the same time.

Here, we're getting the classes, the hours, the hourly rate, and subtotals. The last two need to be formatted as dollars, so we add the dollar sign and change the decimal points to two.

As it loops through, each row will be stored in the variable *invoiceRows*.

Now, we need to start working with the document. First, we need to make a copy of the invoice template.

```
30.        //Create invoice document and get body
31.        const newInvoice = invoiceTemp.makeCopy("Invoice #" + invoiceNo,
32.        fInvoices);
33.        const newInvoiceDoc = DocumentApp.openById(newInvoice.getId());
34.        const body = newInvoiceDoc.getBody();
```

L31-32: We make a copy of the template, name it (e.g. "Invoice #0001") and store it in the invoice folder.

L33: To work with it, we need to open it by its ID.

L34: Then we get its body.

We need to format certain areas of the document and I usually group all this formatting together, so it can be easily found and edited if necessary.

A lot of the formatting uses **DocumentApp.Attribute** followed by the type of formatting and then setting that with the appropriate value. This can all be stored under one style variable as an object. Here's an example of what will be stored:

{FONT_FAMILY=Helvetica Neue, FOREGROUND_COLOR=#FFFFFF, FONT_SIZE=14.0}

So, in this example we have 3 styles, one for the company name (which actually uses two styles), one for the date, and one for the table data.

```
36.        //Set up styles
37.        const s1 = {};
38.        s1[DocumentApp.Attribute.FONT_FAMILY] = 'Helvetica Neue';
39.        s1[DocumentApp.Attribute.FONT_SIZE] = 14;
40.        s1[DocumentApp.Attribute.FOREGROUND_COLOR] = '#FFFFFF';
```

L37: We first set up a variable to store the styles and use the curly brackets, to state it's going to be an object.

L38: To set the font family, we use the style variable then in square brackets add **DocumentApp.Attribute** and then **.FONT_FAMILY**. We then state the font we want in quotes.

L39: To set the font size, we follow the same format, but this time use **.FONT_SIZE** and state the font size number.

L40: For the text colour, we use **.FOREGROUND_COLOR** and then use a hexadecimal number in quotes to represent the colour.

```
42.        const s2 = {};
43.        s2[DocumentApp.Attribute.PADDING_TOP] = 15;
```

L42-43: Let's set up the second style. This will be for the company name and I want to set the top padding. This is the amount of space from this element and the element above it. Basically, I want to set where the company name starts from on the document. This has the same format again, and we use **.PADDING_TOP** to set it.

Finally, let's set up the table styling.

```
45.        const s3 = {};
46.        s3[DocumentApp.Attribute.HORIZONTAL_ALIGNMENT] =
```

```
47.         DocumentApp.HorizontalAlignment.RIGHT;
```

L45-47: Here, we are just going to set the horizontal alignment to the right. We use **.HORIZONTAL_ALIGNMENT** and then rather than just put "right", we have to set it as **DocumentApp.HorizontalAlignment.RIGHT**.

This drove me mad when I was first learning this. I had assumed it would follow the same format as the ones before, but unfortunately not. We'll see some more examples of this later in the book, where the structures are not immediately obvious.

Now, let's start working with the tables. In our template, there are two tables. The first one states the company name we're invoicing, the invoice date and the invoice number.

INVOICE   Widgets Ltd

                                                      18 January 2023

                                                     Invoice No: 0001

```
49.        //Add company name, date & invoice no
50.        const tables = body.getTables();
51.        const table0 = tables[0];
52.        const companyCell = table0.getRow(0).getCell(1);
53.        const dateCell = table0.getRow(1).getCell(1);
54.        const invoiceNoCell = table0.getRow(2).getCell(1);
```

L50: First, get all the tables in the body, which will store them as an array.

L51: Let's get the first table, stored in the first position of the array.

L52: Now, get specific cells in the table. To do so, we need to get the table, then the row number, then the cell number. So, the company name will be in row 1, cell 2. So, here we're getting row(0) and cell(1) (the numbers are array-based).

L53-54: We do the same for the date and invoice number cells. This time getting rows 2 & 3.

```
56.        companyCell.setText(company)
57.                 .setAttributes(s1)
58.                 .setAttributes(s2);
59.        dateCell.setText(date)
60.              .setAttributes(s1);
61.        invoiceNoCell.setText("Invoice No: " + invoiceNo)
62.                 .setAttributes(s1);
```

L56-58: Now, we need to add the text and a bit of styling. First, we use **setText(text)** to add the company name then add the styling using **setAttributes()**. We pass the *s1* styling we created earlier, which will set the font, etc. We're also going to add some padding to the top, so also add the *s2* styling.

L59-60: We then add the date and again use **setText()** to do so. We need to set the styling again, otherwise it will default to the original document styling. So, here we don't want the top padding.

L61-62: Then add the invoice number.

The second table is where the details of the items which have been purchased will be shown. Here, we're going to add multiple items to each of the cells, making it completely dynamic and able to work with however many items we have in our sheet.

CLASSES	HOURS	PRICE / H	SUB TOTAL
Class 01	5.0	$20.00	$100.00
Class 02	10.0	$15.00	$150.00
Class 03	20.0	$20.00	$400.00
		GRAND TOTAL	$650.00

```
64.      //Add invoice items
65.      const table1 = tables[1];
66.      invoiceRows.forEach((invRow) => {
67.        table1.getRow(1).getCell(0)
68.              .appendParagraph(invRow[0]);
69.        table1.getRow(1).getCell(1)
70.              .appendParagraph(invRow[1])
71.              .setAttributes(s3);
72.        table1.getRow(1).getCell(2)
73.              .appendParagraph(invRow[2])
74.              .setAttributes(s3);
75.        table1.getRow(1).getCell(3)
76.              .appendParagraph(invRow[3])
77.              .setAttributes(s3);
78.      });
```

L65: First, we get the table.

Then, we're going to loop through the invoice rows and we're going to append the data as paragraphs within each cell.

L66: So, we use **forEach()** to loop through the invoice rows. *invRow* is the data in each invoice row.

L67-68: We then get the table, the second row, and the first cell and append the invoice row as a paragraph within that cell. The classes are in the first position of the invoice row (see line 25).

L69-78: We do the same for the hours, prices and sub totals. The only difference here is that we are getting cells 2, 3, and 4, and that we are adding right alignment to the numbers.

```
80.      //Calculate and add grand total
81.      const grandTotal = invoiceData.map((r) => {
82.        return r[6];
83.      })
84.      .reduce((runningTotal, subTotal) => {
85.        return runningTotal + subTotal;
86.      });
```

The final part of the table is to add the grand total of items in the invoice.

L81-83: First, by using the **map()** method on the invoice data, we return all the sub-totals using *r[6]*.

L84-86: This will create an array of the sub totals, but we're after the sum of all of them. So, we also use the **reduce()** method. As map is looping through, this will get the current running total and add the next sub-total to it. At the end of the loop, this will store the value in the variable *grandTotal*.

```
88.      table1.getRow(2).getCell(3)
89.          .setText("$" + grandTotal.toFixed(2))
90.          .setAttributes(s3);
91.      }
```

L88-91: Finally, we need to add the grand total to the bottom of the table. We get the table, the third row, and get the fourth cell and set the text, formatting the grand total as we do it, so it is displayed in dollars. We also want to align it to the right, so we add the *s3* attribute.

The menu

To create the menu to run the script, we need to set up an **onOpen()** function.

```
1. function onOpen() {
2.    const ui = SpreadsheetApp.getUi();
3.    ui.createMenu("INVOICE")
4.        .addItem("Make invoice", 'makeInvoice')
5.        .addToUi();
6. }
```

L2-6: Get the spreadsheet UI, create the menu, add the menu item, and then add it to the UI.

Let's make an example and see what it looks like.

INVOICES				Invoice to make:		0002 ▾
Invoice number	Company	Date	Classes	Hourly rate	Hours	Sub total
0001	Widgets Ltd	18/01/2023	Class 01	$20.00	5	$100.00
0001	Widgets Ltd	18/01/2023	Class 02	$15.00	10	$150.00
0001	Widgets Ltd	18/01/2023	Class 03	$20.00	20	$400.00
0002	Gizmos Inc	19/01/2023	Class 01	$20.00	10	$200.00
0002	Gizmos Inc	19/01/2023	Class 02	$15.00	40	$600.00

We select the invoice number to make in cell G1.

INVOICE

Make invoice

Then from the INVOICE menu, select 'Make invoice'. This then creates the document and stores it in the folder we want.

BAZROBERTS

INVOICE		Gizmos Inc
		19 January 2023
		Invoice No: 0002

CLASSES	HOURS	PRICE / H	SUB TOTAL
Class 01	10.0	$20.00	$200.00
Class 02	40.0	$15.00	$600.00
		GRAND TOTAL	$800.00

PAYMENT TERMS

To be paid within 30 days of receipt.

ADDRESS

123 Main Street • Big Town, USA • 12345

As we can see, it's added the company, date and invoice number. Then, below it's added the invoice items from the sheet and calculated the grand total.

5: Making a document from scratch
-Invoice

In this chapter, we're going to dynamically create an invoice from information stored in a Google Sheet without the need of a template. It can be more complicated to create but it also allows for complete flexibility.

Overview

1) The user will fill in the invoice data into the Google Sheet with each line detailing a particular product purchased.
2) They will then select the invoice number they want to create and run the program from the menu.
3) This will create an invoice in a Google Doc and store it in a specific folder.
4) The invoice will contain:
    a. the company logo in the header;
    b. the company name, invoice number and invoice date;
    c. the order date, a list of the products ordered and a description of each;
    d. a table with the prices, quantities, sub totals and grand total;
    e. the invoice due date;
    f. the company's contact details in the footer.
5) It will also add a link to that document in the Google Sheet.

Key learning points

1) How to use regular expressions to format data.
2) How to calculate a future date.
3) How to add a logo into a header and position the image.
4) How to set up multiple styles.
5) How to work with different script files.
6) How to add bolded and normal text in the same line.
7) How to add lists dynamically.
8) How to add a table, rows, and cells dynamically.
9) And finally, how to add a table to a footer.

This also builds on some of the learning points from the previous chapter.

First, let's look at the sheet and the data we'll be entering and using.

Sheet

	A	B	C	D	E	F	G	H
1	**INVOICES**				Invoice to make:		**0001** ▾	
2	**Invoice number**	**Company**	**Date**	**Products**	**Unit Price**	**Quantity**	**Sub total**	**LINK**
3	0001	Widgets Ltd	29/06/2023	Product A	$100.00	1,000	$100,000.00	LINK
4	0001	Widgets Ltd	29/06/2023	Product B	$250.00	100	$25,000.00	
5	0001	Widgets Ltd	29/06/2023	Product C	$1,000.00	15	$15,000.00	

Invoice Example

BazRoberts

INVOICE

COMPANY: Widgets Ltd

INVOICE NUMBER: #0001

DATE: 29/06/2023

The following products were ordered on 18 June 2023

1. Product A - Red Widget with matching case.
2. Product B - Solar-powered blue widget
3. Product C - 100% recycled green widget

Products	Unit Price	Quantity	Sub total
Product A	$100.00	1,000	$100,000.00
Product B	$250.00	100	$25,000.00
Product C	$1,000.00	15	$15,000.00
		Grand total:	**$140,000.00**

Payment is due on **29/07/2023**.

Thank you for your custom.

Baz Roberts

E: baz@bazroberts.com   T: 123456789   W: www.bazroberts.com

The code
This project is divided into 9 separate scripts files. I've divided it up like that as it's quite a long project and each script file does a specific part of the program although most are under 20 lines long, so they are easy to read and understand, rather than being part of one long script. It's also an opportunity to show how variables can be passed between functions.

This script is bound to the spreadsheet where we enter the invoice details into.

Script 1
Main make invoice script

The first part of the script is very similar to what we saw in the previous chapter.

```
1. function makeInvoice() {
2. //Get invoice data
3. const ss = SpreadsheetApp.getActiveSpreadsheet();
4. const sh = ss.getSheetByName('INVOICES');
5. const fInvoices = DriveApp.getFolderById('FOLDER ID');
6. const timeZone = Session.getScriptTimeZone();
7. const data = sh.getDataRange().getValues();
8. const invoiceNumb = data[0][6];
```

L1: Open the function

L3-4: First, let's get the spreadsheet and the sheet called INVOICES.

L5: Then let's get the folder we're going to store the invoices in. Add your folder ID here.

L6: Get the time zone to format the date later on.

L7: Then get all the data on the sheet.

L8: Finally, we get the invoice number we've selected to make.

Now, we need to get only the data for the invoice we've selected.

```
10.     //Filter data by invoice selected
11.     data.splice(0, 2);
12.     const invoiceData = data.filter((row) => {
13.         return row[0] === invoiceNumb;
14.     });
```

L11: We remove the first 2 rows with the **splice()** method.

L12-14: Then, we filter the rows of data by the invoice number (which is in column A) and store it in the variable *invoiceData*.

```
16.        //Get company & dates and format data
17.        const company = invoiceData[0][1];
18.        const orderDate1 = invoiceData[0][2];
19.        const invoiceNo = ('0000' + invoiceNumb).slice(-4);
```

L17-18: Get the company and order date from the first row which matches the invoice number.

L19: I want the invoice number to be a 4-digit number, so we add 4 zeros at the start and then slice the last 4 digits.

```
21.        //Format dates & calculate due date
22.        const todaysDate = new Date();
23.        const orderDate = Utilities.formatDate(orderDate1,
24.        timeZone, 'd MMMMM yyyy');
25.        const todaysDate2 = Utilities.formatDate(todaysDate,
26.        timeZone, 'dd/MM/yyyy');
27.        const dueDateMSecs = new Date(todaysDate.getTime()
28.        + (30 * 86400000));
29.        const dueDate = Utilities.formatDate(dueDateMSecs,
30.        timeZone, 'dd/MM/yyyy');
```

We need to calculate the invoice due date, which will be 30 days from today.

L22: First, we get today's date by getting a new date object.

L23-24: The order date we got from the sheet and then we format it.

L25-26: We format today's date and store it in a new variable.

L27-28: To calculate the due date, we convert today's date into milliseconds by using **getTime()** on the date, then we add 30 days. One day is 86,400,000 milliseconds and multiply that by 30 days.

L29-30: We then convert those milliseconds into a formatted date which we'll add to the invoice.

Now, we get the product information: the product name, the unit price, the quantity, and the sub total.

```
32.        //Get product info and format
33.        const productInfo = invoiceData.map((rw) => {
34.           return [rw[3],
35.           "$" + rw[4].toFixed(2)
```

```
36.                    .replace(/\d(?=(\d{3})+\.)/g, '$&,'),
37.         rw[5].toFixed(0)
38.              .replace(/-{0,1}(\d)(?=(\d\d\d)+$)/g, '$1,'),
39.         "$" + rw[6].toFixed(2)
40.                   .replace(/\d(?=(\d{3})+\.)/g, '$&,')];
41.       });
```

L33: We use the **map()** method to loop through the invoice data. *rw* is each row of data.

L34: We return the 4 pieces of information we want, starting with the product name in column D.

L35-36: Then we get the unit price and need to format it into dollars with 2 decimal places and also, as these could be over 1,000, I want to add commas to separate the thousands.

So, going from left to right, we add the dollar sign, get the unit price and add 2 decimal places with **toFixed(2)**, then we add a potential thousand comma with a regular expression combined with the **replace()** method.

The part in between the brackets is the regular expression: (/\d(?=(\d{3})+\.)/g, '$&,') It looks scary but I have a collection of these which I have found on the Net and I just copy and paste it into my code.

L37-38: This line gets the quantity and as it's a quantity not a currency, we don't need 2 decimal places, so use the regular expression /-{0,1}(\d)(?=(\d\d\d)+$)/g, '$1,'.

L39-40: The final one is the sub total, which is similar to lines 35-36.

This is then all stored in the *productInfo* variable as an array, with each row containing 4 items.

Now, it's time to start making the document.

```
43.       //Create invoice document & move to folder
44.       const newInvoice = DocumentApp.create("Invoice #" + invoiceNo);
45.       const newInvID = newInvoice.getId();
46.       const newInvoiceDocF = DriveApp.getFileById(newInvID);
47.       newInvoiceDocF.moveTo(fInvoices);
```

L44: We create a blank document with **DocumentApp.create()** and give it a filename.

By default, it is created in our My Drive, so we need to move it to the invoices folder.

L45: First, we get the new document's ID.

L46: Then we get the file by its ID using the **DriveApp**.

L47: Then we move it into the invoices folder.

The body needs to line up well with the header logo I'm using, so we need to set up the body margins.

```
49.      //Open doc and set up body
50.      const newInvoiceDoc = DocumentApp.openById(newInvID);
51.      const body = newInvoiceDoc.getBody();
52.      body.setMarginTop(150);
53.      body.setMarginLeft(70);
54.      body.setMarginRight(70);
```

L54: To work with the document, we open it by its ID.

L55: Then we get the document's body.

L56: To set the margin from the top of the document we use **setMarginTop(number)** on the body.

L57-58: We then set the left and right margins too, with **setMarginLeft()** and **setMarginRight()**.

```
56.      //Run other functions
57.      const style = getStyles();
```

L57: I've stored the style in a separate script file under a function called **getStyles()**. So, we call that function and what is returned is stored in the variable *style*.

We'll look at the **getStyles()** function later on.

The next few lines are calls to different functions stored in different script files. This helps keep our code clean and easy to follow. I'll explain each of the scripts later in this chapter (scripts 2 to 9).

```
59.      addLogo(newInvoiceDoc);
60.
61.      addInvoiceDetails(body, style, company, invoiceNo, todaysDate2);
62.
63.      addListOfProducts(body, orderDate, style, productInfo);
```

```
64.
65.        const table = addTable(body, sh, style, productInfo);
66.
67.        addGrandTotal(invoiceData, table, productInfo, style);
68.
69.        addLastTextAndFooter(body, style, dueDate, newInvoiceDoc);
```

L59: Next we will add the logo in the header by calling the **addLogo()** function and passing the invoice document we've just created as a parameter.

L61: Then we'll add the invoice details, like company name, invoice number, etc. Here we need to pass the body, as we'll be editing it and also the *style* variable as we need to use that.

L63: We then add the list of products that have been purchased, again passing the parameters that we'll need in that function.

L65: We then add the table of products with their prices, quantities, etc. Note, as we will need to work more on the table in the next function, we need to return the table, and it is stored in the variable *table*.

L67: Next, we add the grand total to the table and this is why we needed that *table* variable.

L69: The last function to call is **addLastTextAndFooter()** which adds some text after the table and also adds the footer.

The final part of this script is to add a link to the file back on our Google Sheet.

```
71.        //Add document link to sheet
72.        const indexNo = data.map((row) => {
73.          return row[0];
74.        })
75.        .indexOf(invoiceNumb);
76.        sh.getRange(indexNo + 3, 8)
77.          .setFormula('=HYPERLINK("' + newInvoiceDoc.getUrl()
78.          + '","LINK")');
79.        }
```

L72-74: Using **map()** we loop through all the data, initially returning the invoice number in column A.

L75: We then chain **indexOf()** to it to find the position of the invoice number we're looking for. Note, **indexOf()** will return the first position it finds that matches the criteria, so even though we may have multiple rows with the same invoice number, it'll return the first one it finds.

L76-78: We then get the sheet and the range using the index number it's just found and add 3 to get the row number (position 0 would be row 3 on the sheet). Then we add a hyperlink to the cell in column H. We use **setFormula(formula, text)** to set the HYPERLINK formula to the document URL and then rather than show a long URL, we display the word LINK in the cell.

L79: Close the function.

Script 2
Set up the styles

In line 57 in script 1, we called the function **getStyles()**. Let's go through that function.

```
1.  function getStyles() {
2.        const style0 = {};
3.        style0[DocumentApp.Attribute.FONT_FAMILY] = 'Helvetica Neue';
4.
5.        const style1 = {};
6.        style1[DocumentApp.Attribute.FONT_SIZE] = 30;
7.        style1[DocumentApp.Attribute.BOLD] = true;
8.        style1[DocumentApp.Attribute.LINE_SPACING] = 1.5;
9.
10.       const style2 = {};
11.       style2[DocumentApp.Attribute.FONT_SIZE] = 12;
12.       style2[DocumentApp.Attribute.BOLD] = true;
13.       style2[DocumentApp.Attribute.LINE_SPACING] = 2;
14.
15.       const style3 = {};
16.       style3[DocumentApp.Attribute.FONT_SIZE] = 12;
17.       style3[DocumentApp.Attribute.BOLD] = false;
18.       style3[DocumentApp.Attribute.LINE_SPACING] = 2;
19.
20.       const style4 = {};
21.       style4[DocumentApp.Attribute.FONT_SIZE] = 12;
22.       style4[DocumentApp.Attribute.BOLD] = false;
23.
24.       const style5 = {};
25.       style5[DocumentApp.Attribute.FONT_SIZE] = 11;
26.       style5[DocumentApp.Attribute.FONT_FAMILY] = 'Comfortaa';
27.       style5[DocumentApp.Attribute.FOREGROUND_COLOR] = '#FFFFFF';
```

L1: Open the function.

L2: Set up the variable to hold the first style as an object.

L3: In this style, we're just going to set the font. To do so, we get the style variable and in the square brackets add **DocumentApp.Attribute** and then add **.FONT_FAMILY** to it. We then state the font we want.

L5-27: The next styles follow a similar pattern, where we use the **DocumentApp.Attribute** and add the property we want and the value.

Then we set up the three different horizontal alignments, left, center, and right.

```
29.        const style6 = {};
30.        style6[DocumentApp.Attribute.HORIZONTAL_ALIGNMENT] =
31.        DocumentApp.HorizontalAlignment.LEFT;
32.        const style7 = {};
33.        style7[DocumentApp.Attribute.HORIZONTAL_ALIGNMENT] =
34.        DocumentApp.HorizontalAlignment.CENTER;
35.        const style8 = {};
36.        style8[DocumentApp.Attribute.HORIZONTAL_ALIGNMENT] =
37.        DocumentApp.HorizontalAlignment.RIGHT;
```

They follow a similar format as before, but you can see that we have to use **DocumentApp.HorizontalAlignment** to then set the alignments.

```
41.        return [style0, style1, style2, style3, style4,
42.        style5, style6, style7, style8];
43.        }
```

L41-42: We then return all these styles in an array format.

This is then sent to the variable *style* back on line 57 in script 1.

Script 3
Add the logo in the header

In this part, we're going to add the logo in the top left-hand corner of the document.

In script 1, line 59, we called the function **addLogo()**.

```
1. function addLogo(newInvoiceDoc) {
```

```
2.    //Get the logo and create the header
3.    const logo = DriveApp.getFileById('FILE ID').getBlob();
4.    newInvoiceDoc.addHeader();
5.    const header = newInvoiceDoc.getHeader();
```

L1: Open the function and pass the new invoice document as a parameter.

L3: We get the logo we're going to use, which is an image stored on our Drive. We get it by its file ID and then get the blob, which is the data to make it.

Note, to get an image's ID, you need to open it in your Drive in a new window, not just the preview of it.

L4: As we want to add this to the header, we first must add a header, as by default a document doesn't have one. To do so, we get the document and use **addHeader()**.

L5: Once added, we can get the header to work with it.

By default, the image will be positioned on the page as above, but I want to add it into the corner of the page. So, we'll need to set the position and offset it from its normal position. This is why we use **addPostionedImage()**.

```
7.  //Add the logo and position
8.  const hparas = header.getParagraphs();
9.  hparas[0].addPositionedImage(logo)
10.         .setTopOffset(-30)
11.         .setLeftOffset(-70);
12.      }
```

L8: First, we get the paragraphs in the header.

L9: Then using the first paragraph, we'll add the image using **addPositionedImage(image blob)**.

L10-11: We can then chain the offset moving it towards the top, using **setTopOffset()** and a negative number and do the same for moving it to the left using **setLeftOffset()** and again a negative number.

Script 4
Add the company, invoice number and date

Here, we're going to add some of the invoice details.

INVOICE

COMPANY: Widgets Ltd

INVOICE NUMBER: #0001

DATE: 29/06/2023

In line 61, we called the function **addInvoiceDetails()**.

```
1. function addInvoiceDetails(body, style, company, invoiceNo,
2.    todaysDate2) {
3.    //Add Invoice details
4.    body.setAttributes(style[0]);
5.    body.appendParagraph("INVOICE")
6.       .setAttributes(style[1]);
```

L1-2: We open the function and pass the body, the style, the company name, invoice number, and date as parameters.

L4: We set the font for all the body, by setting the attribute *style0*, which we set up in script 2 and is the first style in the array.

L5-6: Here, we're going to add the text "INVOICE", simply by appending it as a paragraph and style it.

```
8. const text1 = body.appendParagraph("COMPANY: ")
9.                .setAttributes(style[2]);
10.      text1.appendText(company)
11.          .setAttributes(style[3]);
```

L8-9: We then append the text "COMPANY: " and style it.

L10-11: This time I want to add another piece of text on the same line. So, we can't use *appendParagraph* as that would add a new line, so we need to use **appendText()** on the text we've just added. Plus, we can style it differently from the previous text.

```
13.      const text2 = body.appendParagraph("INVOICE NUMBER: ")
14.                .setAttributes(style[2]);
```

```
15.          text2.appendText("#" + invoiceNo)
16.              .setAttributes(style[3]);
17.
18.          const text3 = body.appendParagraph("DATE: ")
19.                          .setAttributes(style[2]);
20.          text3.appendText(todaysDate2)
21.              .setAttributes(style[3]);
```

L13-21: We do the same thing for the invoice number and date.

```
23.          //Add horizontal rule and empty row
24.          body.appendHorizontalRule();
25.          body.appendParagraph("");
26.        }
```

L24: I then want to add a horizontal rule, which we simply append.

L25: Plus, I want a blank line under it, to give a bit of spacing between this and the next section. We just append an empty paragraph.

Script 5
Add the list of products and their descriptions

Here, we're going to add the list of products in the order, along with their descriptions.

The following products were ordered on 29 June 2023

1. Product A - Red Widget with matching case.
2. Product B - Solar-powered blue widget
3. Product C - 100% recycled green widget

In script 1, line 63, we called the function **addInvoiceDetails()**.

```
1. function addListOfProducts(body, orderDate, style, productInfo) {
2.    //Product descriptions
3.    const products = ["Product A", "Product B", "Product C"];
4.    const prodDescs = ["Red Widget with matching case.",
5.                       "Solar-powered blue widget",
6.                       "100% recycled green widget"];
```

L1: Open the function and pass the body, order date, styles, and products as parameters.

L3: Here, we have an array of all the possible products.

L4-6: In *prodDescs* we have an array of the descriptions of all those products. Note, these need to be in the same order as the *products* array.

```
8.  //Add list & descs
9.  body.appendParagraph("The following products were ordered on "
10.        + orderDate).setAttributes(style[3]);
```

L9-10: First, I want to add a line confirming when the products were ordered. So, we append a paragraph and add the order date to it, then set the styling.

```
12.       productInfo.forEach((r) => {
13.          const desc = prodDescs[products.indexOf(r[0])];
14.          body.appendListItem(r[0] + " - " + desc);
15.       });
16.          body.appendParagraph("");
17.       }
```

L12: Then we loop through the *productInfo* array, which contains the products that have been ordered. Each row of info will be stored in *r*.

L13: As we loop through, we get the position of the product in the *products* array, by using **indexOf()** and getting the first item in the *r* variable. Then we store that in the variable *desc*.

L14: To make a bullet list, we append a list item and pass the product name and the description to it. As this loops round, it will add multiple bullet points to create our list.

L16: I've added an empty line for spacing.

Script 6
Add the table data

Here, we're going to set up the table which contains the products ordered, the unit prices, quantities, and sub totals.

Products	Unit Price	Quantity	Sub total
Product A	$100.00	1,000	$100,000.00
Product B	$250.00	100	$25,000.00
Product C	$1,000.00	15	$15,000.00
		Grand total:	$140,000.00

In script 1, line 65, we called the function **addTable()**.

```
1. function addTable(body, sh, style, productInfo) {
2.    //Add table and header row
3.    const table = body.appendTable();
4.    const headerRow = table.appendTableRow();
5.    const tableHeaders = sh.getRange(2, 4, 1, 4).getValues();
```

L1: We open the function and pass the body, sheet, styles and product info as parameters.

L3: First we append the table to the body.

L4: Then we append the first table row, which will be the header row.

L5: Then we get the data from the sheet we want to add to the header row cells.

Then we add the header data and format the header row.

```
7. //Add header data and format
8. tableHeaders[0].forEach((hr) => {
9.    const headerCell = headerRow.appendTableCell()
10.                              .setBackgroundColor('#ea9999')
11.                              .setAttributes(style[2])
12.                              .setText(hr);
13.        headerCell.getChild(0).setAttributes(style[7]);
14.    });
```

L8: We now need to loop through the header data. Note, as this is a 2D array, we have to get the first row, i.e. *tableHeaders[0]* and then loop through it to get each cell, in *hr*.

L9: To the header row we will append a table cell, which will add a table cell horizontally across the table row.

L10: To the header cell, let's add a salmon background colour.

L11: Then we can add the style 2 which will add bolding, etc.

L12: Then we add the cell text. Using **setText()** and *hr*.

L13: Finally, we will add center alignment. Note, here we need to get the first child of the header cell, we can't just chain it to the header cell as we did with the above formatting.

Now, we're going to add the table rows with the product data. We're going to add alternate row colours, and then add the data in the table and also the formatting. There are two loops, one to add the rows and one to add the cells in each row.

```
16.        //Add table rows and cells
17.        let color;
18.        productInfo.forEach((tr, r) => {
19.          const tableRow = table.appendTableRow();
20.          //Alternate row colouring
21.          if (r % 2 === 0) {
22.            color = '#efefef';
23.          } else {
24.            color = '#ffffff';
25.          }
```

L17: First, we set up a variable to store the row background colour. We need this to be before the **forEach** iteration so that it is visible in the section below.

L18: First, we set up the loop to go through the product info.

L19: Then in each loop we append a table row.

L21: I want to add a light grey colour to every other row. So, we use the modulo of 2, which if it is an even number will be zero, i.e. an even number divided by 2 will result in a number without any decimal point.

L22: If the modulo of 2 is zero we set the colour as light grey.

L23-25: If not, we set it as white.

Now, we format the cell and add the cell text.

```
27.        //Add product info and style
28.        productInfo[r].forEach((tc, c) => {
29.          const tableCell = tableRow.appendTableCell()
30.                                  .setAttributes(style[4])
31.                                  .setBackgroundColor(color)
32.                                  .setText(tc);
```

L28-29: We loop through the cells per row (r) and append the table cells.

L30-32: Then we format the cells, first adding style 4 which removes the bolding, setting the cell background colour, either the light grey or white, as set up above, and finally, to add the text in the cell.

So, giving an example, this will add the second row, then add Product A, then $100.00, then $1,000, and then $100,000. Then it will add the third row, and the cells, and so on.

Finally, we align the cells.

```
34.         //The first cell we align to the left
35.         //And the others to the right
36.         if (c === 0) {
37.           tableCell.getChild(0).setAttributes(style[6]);
38.         } else {
39.           tableCell.getChild(0).setAttributes(style[8]);
40.         }
41.       });
42.     });
43.     return table;
44.   }
```

L36-37: If the cell is the first one, we align it to the left (style 6).

L38-40: Otherwise, we align the cells to the right (style 8).

L41-42: We close the two **forEach()** loops.

L43: Then we return the table we have just made.

Script 7
Add the grand total to the table

The final part of the table is to add the row with the grand total of the products purchased.

Product C	$1,000.00	15	$15,000.00
		Grand total:	**$140,000.00**

In script 1, line 67, we called the function **addGrandTotal()**.

```
1. function addGrandTotal(invoiceData, table, productInfo, style) {
2.   //Calculate grand total
3.   const grandTotal = invoiceData.map((r) => {
4.     return r[6];
5.   })
6.     .reduce((runningTotal, subTotal) => {
7.       return runningTotal + subTotal;
8.     });
```

L1: Open the function and pass the invoice data, the table, the product info and the styles as parameters.

First, we're going to calculate the grand total from the sub totals. This is basically the same code we saw in the last chapter.

L3-5: First, by using the **map()** method on the invoice data, we return all the sub-totals using *r[6]*.

L6-8: This will create an array of the sub totals, but we're after the sum of all of them. So, we also use the **reduce()** method. As map is looping through, this will get the current running total and add the next sub-total to it. At the end of the loop this will store the value in the variable *grandTotal*.

```
10.        //Add grand total cells
11.        const gtRow = table.appendTableRow();
12.
13.        productInfo[0].forEach((tc, c) => {
14.          const tableCell = gtRow.appendTableCell();
15.          tableCell.setBackgroundColor('#d9d9d9')
16.                  .setAttributes(style[2]);
```

L11: Next, we append a table row and call it *gtRow*.

Next, we add the grand total to the table.

L13: We use the *productInfo* row, just to loop though the same number of table columns to maintain the same number of columns in our table.

L14: Then as we loop through we append a table cell.

L15-16: Then we add a darker grey background colour and add style 2 to add bolding and line spacing.

Here, I want to align the text to the left and for the grand total format it as a currency.

```
18.        if (c === 2) {
19.          tableCell.setText('Grand total: ');
20.          tableCell.getChild(0).setAttributes(style[8]);
21.        } else if (c === 3) {
22.          tableCell.setText("$" + grandTotal
23.                  .toFixed(2).replace(/\d(?=(\d{3})+\.)/g, '$&,'));
24.          tableCell.getChild(0).setAttributes(style[8]);
25.        }
26.      });
27.    }
```

L18-20: If the table cell is the third one, we add the text "Grand total: " and align it to the left.

L21-25: If the table cell is the fourth one, then we add the currency format, including adding a comma if it's more than 1000, and align it to the left.

L26-27: We close the **forEach()** loop and the function.

Script 8
Add the last piece of text and the footer

Here, we add when the payment is due, and a thank you note.

Payment is due on **29/07/2023**.

Thank you for your custom.

Baz Roberts

Plus, we add a footer with our contact details.

E: baz@bazroberts.com	T: 123456789	W: www.bazroberts.com

In script 1, line 69, we called the function **addGrandTotal()**.

```
1.  function addLastTextAndFooter(body, style,
2.      dueDate, newInvoiceDoc) {
3.      //Add due date
4.      const text4 = body.appendParagraph("Payment is due on ")
5.                      .setAttributes(style[3]);
6.      text4.appendText(dueDate).setAttributes(style[2]);
7.      text4.appendText(".").setAttributes(style[3]);
```

L1-2: Open the function and pass the body, the styles, the due date, and the invoice document.

First, we add the text which contains the due date.

L4-5: We append the paragraph and style it.

L6: We then need to append the due date to the paragraph and style it.

L7: As the due date was in bold, we add the full stop without bolding.

```
9.  //Add thank you & name
10.         body.appendParagraph("Thank you for your custom.")
11.             .setAttributes(style[3]);
```

```
12.        body.appendParagraph("Baz Roberts")
13.            .setAttributes(style[3]);
14.        body.appendHorizontalRule();
```

L10-13: We append and style the paragraphs.

L14: We add a horizontal line.

The final part of the invoice is to add the footer with our contact details.

```
16.    //Add footer
17.    newInvoiceDoc.addFooter();
18.    const footer = newInvoiceDoc.getFooter();
19.    const tableF = footer.insertTable(0);
20.    const tableRowF = tableF.appendTableRow();
21.    const footerText =
22.        ["E: baz@bazroberts.com",
23.         "T: 123456789",
24.         "W: www.bazroberts.com"];
```

L17: First, we add the footer to the document, using **addFooter()**.

L18: Then we get the footer to work with it.

L19: We're going to a table with 1 row and 3 columns. So first, we add the table. Here, I've used **insertTable()** and added it to the child Index 0, instead of **appendTable()**. In this case, it's the same, I just wanted to show you that you can insert a table into a specific position.

L20: Then we append a table row.

L21-24: Then we set up an array that contains the text of the 3 cells we want to add.

Now, we'll add the table cells and the formatting.

```
26.    footerText.forEach((fText) => {
27.      const fCell = tableRowF.appendTableCell()
28.                        .setBackgroundColor('#cc0000')
29.                        .setAttributes(style[5])
30.                        .setWidth(150)
31.                        .setText(fText);
32.      fCell.getChild(0).setAttributes(style[7]);
33.    });
34.    }
```

L26-32: We'll loop through the *footerText* array and will append a table cell, set the background colour to red, the text to white and change the font to 'Comfortaa', set the cell widths, add the contact details, and centre the texts.

L33-34: We close the **forEach()** loop and close the function.

Script 9
Set up the menu

Here, we'll add a menu to the Sheet to be able to run the program. This will add it automatically when the sheet is opened, by using the function name **onOpen()**.

```
1. function onOpen() {
2.   const ui = SpreadsheetApp.getUi();
3.   ui.createMenu("INVOICE")
4.     .addItem("Make invoice", 'makeInvoice')
5.     .addToUi();
6. }
```

L1: We open the function.

L2: We get the spreadsheet UI.

L3-6: We create the menu, add the menu item and add it to the UI.

Let's add an example and run the program. Here, I've added a second invoice (0002).

INVOICES				Invoice to make:		0002 ⌄	
Invoice number	Company	Date	Products	Unit Price	Quantity	Sub total	LINK
0001	Widgets Ltd	29/06/2023	Product A	$100.00	1,000	$100,000.00	LINK
0001	Widgets Ltd	29/06/2023	Product B	$250.00	100	$25,000.00	
0001	Widgets Ltd	29/06/2023	Product C	$1,000.00	15	$15,000.00	
0002	Gizmos Inc	30/06/2023	Product B	$250.00	100	$25,000.00	LINK
0002	Gizmos Inc	30/06/2023	Product C	$20.00	2,000	$40,000.00	

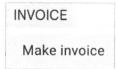

We run the program from the menu. As we can see it's created an invoice with the details from the sheet. It also added a link to it on the sheet.

BazRoberts

INVOICE

COMPANY: Gizmos Inc

INVOICE NUMBER: #0002

DATE: 30/06/2023

The following products were ordered on 30 June 2023

1. Product B - Solar-powered blue widget
2. Product C - 100% recycled green widget

Products	Unit Price	Quantity	Sub total
Product B	$250.00	100	$25,000.00
Product C	$20.00	2,000	$40,000.00
		Grand total:	**$65,000.00**

Payment is due on **30/07/2023**.

Thank you for your custom.

Baz Roberts

6: Making student reports with progress bars

In this chapter, we're going to create individual reports for students at a company who are having English classes at an academy. The data is entered into a Google Sheet and then the program creates the individual reports using Google Docs as a basis.

Overview

1) The teacher will fill in the data on the Google Sheet, with one line per student.
2) The report will contain:
   a. the student's group number;
   b. the language studied and the group's level;
   c. the teacher's name;
   d. the student's name and email address;
   e. the period studied;
   f. marks out of 10 for speaking, etc;
   g. the exam mark (and if there isn't one to deal with it)
   h. their attendance percentage
   i. and the student's level and progression
3) The teacher will then select which reports they want to make and then run the program from the menu.
4) This will create an individual report from a template, using the data from the Sheet, stored in a specific folder as a Google Doc.
5) It will then add links to the reports on the Sheet and reset the Make report column.

Key learning points

1) How to manipulate data from the sheet into the format required for the report.
2) How to work with tables, including styling them to create progress bars.
3) How to check for empty cells in a row on a sheet.
4) How to convert numbers on the sheet to bar lengths on the report.

First, let's look at the sheet and the data we'll be entering and using.

Sheet

	A	B	C	D	E	F	G
1	**Widgets Ltd**						
2	**Group**	**Language**	**Class Level**	**Teacher**	**Students**	**Email**	**Period**
3	01	English	A1	Ian Teacher	John Len	email2@email.com	oct19-jun20
4	01	English	A1	Ian Teacher	Paul Mac	email2@email.com	oct19-jun20
5	02	English	A2	Mercedes Profesora	Ringo Sta	email3@email.com	oct19-jun20
6	02	English	A2	Mercedes Profesora	George Har	email4@email.com	oct19-jun20
7	02	English	A2	Mercedes Profesora	Wilma Flint	email5@email.com	oct19-jun20

H	I	J	K	L	M	N	O
Speaking	**Listening**	**Writing**	**Reading**	**Grammar**	**Vocabulary**	**Exam Mark**	**Attendance**
6	7	8	9	6	6	6.8	50%
9	6	8	8	8	10	9.2	75%
4	4	X	6	4	6	5.5	50%
8	8	8	6	6	10	7.5	90%
6	8	10	8	8	6	8.6	90%

Key:	9-10: Excellent	3-4: OK
	7-8: Very good	1-2: Insufficient
	5-6: Good	X: Not evaluated

P	Q	R	S	T	U	V	W	X
Student Level	**P**	**Progression**					**Links**	**Make**
A1	3	X	X	X			REPORT	Made
A2	2	X	X				REPORT	Made
A2	2	X	X				REPORT	Made
A2	4	X	X	X	X			N
A2	4	X	X	X	X			N

	0: Starting the level
	5: Has finished the level

Each row contains the details of a student. We have:

-Their group, language, class level, teacher's name, their name and email address, and the period of the report.

-Then we have the marks out of ten for the various skills and language areas.

-Followed by their exam mark, attendance, their level and their progress within that level.

-Finally, we have a part to store links to their individual reports, and the last two columns are to tell the program whether to make a report or not.

Report

The sheet data for each student is converted into this report.

PROGRESS REPORT

Name:	John Len	Teacher:	Ian Teacher
Company:	Widgets Ltd	Language:	English
Period:	oct22-jun23	Group:	01

For the level	Insufficient	OK	Good	Very Good	Excellent
Speaking:			X		
Listening:				X	
Writing:				X	
Reading:					X
Grammar:			X		
Vocabulary:			X		

Overall Level:	A1				
Progression:	>	>	>		

Exam Mark:	6.8 / 10	Attendance:	50%

BARRIE ROBERTS

Director of Studies

Note, how the marks out of 10 are converted into progress bars relating to Good, etc. The progression number is also converted into a bar. Then at the bottom we add the exam mark and show that it's out of 10.

The code
The code is split into 5 script files.

1-makeReports.gs
2-setupData.gs
3-createReports.gs
4-addToSheet.gs
5-onOpen.gs

We have the main function called **makeReports()**, then we have one which will set up the data format, then create the report using that data, then add the link and update the make column. Plus, we have a function which will add a menu to run the program from.

Script 1

Get the spreadsheet data, the rows that need making, and check all the data has been entered in those rows.

```
1. function makeReports() {
2.     //Get data
3.     const ss = SpreadsheetApp.getActiveSpreadsheet();
4.     const sheet = ss.getActiveSheet();
5.     const data = sheet.getDataRange().getValues();
6.     const company = data[0][0];
7.     data.splice(0, 2);
```

L1: Open the function.

L3-5: Get the spreadsheet, the active sheet and all the values on it.

L6: Get the company name from cell A1.

L7: Then remove the first two rows from the data, to leave us with the table data.

```
9.         //Get report template and report folder IDs
10.        const reportTemplate = DriveApp.getFileById('FILE ID');
11.        const reportFolder = DriveApp.getFolderById('FOLDER ID');
```

L10-11: Get the template we're going to use and the folder we're going to store the reports in by their IDs.

```
13.        //Filter rows by "Y" in Make column & get row indexes
14.        const reportRows = data.map((rr, index) => {
15.          rr.push(index);
16.          return rr;
17.        })
18.          .filter((rr) => {
19.            return rr[23] === "Y";
20.          });
```

L14: Using the **map()** method, we iterate through the data and return one row at a time in *rr*.

L15: I want to store the index of the rows being added to *reportRows* to be able to get the row number on the sheet. We can do that by adding the value onto the end of the row array using **push**.

L16-17: Return the rows and store them in *reportRows*.

L18-20: We then use the **filter()** method to filter the rows and only return the row if column X (position 23 in the array) is equal to "Y". I.e. We want to make a report for that row. If true, this is then stored in the variable *reportRows*.

This is a useful chunk of code to keep, as it's a quick and easy way to filter your rows of data by a certain value in that data. The only line that you don't usually need is line 15.

```
22.        const numOfReports = reportRows.length;
23.        let reportMade = false;
```

L22: Getting the length of *reportRows* will give us how many reports we're going to make. We'll use that to notify the user of the progress of making the reports.

L23: I want to tell the user if reports were made or not, so here we're going to set up a variable to do that and set it initially as false. If any reports are made, this will change to true.

Next, I've added a check to make sure all the data has been completed in the rows we want to make. If there are any cells missing it will add a "cell missing info" message in the row that is missing data.

```
25.        //Loop thru rows to be made
26.        reportRows.forEach((rRow, num) => {
27.          const rowNo = rRow[25] + 3;
28.          //Check to see if any cells up to column Q are empty,
29.          //if so, add msg on sheet, if not, make report
30.          if (rRow.indexOf("") > -1 && rRow.indexOf("") < 17) {
31.            sheet.getRange(rowNo, 23).setValue("Cell missing info");
32.          }
```

L26: Iterate through the *reportRows* array. I'm using the index *num* to keep track of how many reports are being made.

L27: Get the row number of the current row by getting the index we stored earlier and adding 3 to get the row number on the sheet.

L30: Here we check to see if there are any empty cells between the first one to column Q (the 17th one). We do that by using **indexOf()** and seeing if it finds any blank cells. If it does, the number will be greater than -1, if it doesn't, it will be -1.

L31: If it does find a blank cell, it adds the text "Cell missing info" in column W.

```
34.        else {
35.          const reportData = setUpData(rRow); //Script 2
36.
37.          const report = createReport(company, reportTemplate,
38.           reportFolder, reportData);  //Script 3
39.
40.          reportMade = addToSheet(report, num, ss, sheet,
41.          numOfReports, rowNo);  //Script 4
42.        }
43.      });
```

L34: If it doesn't find any blanks then it will go on and make the report.

L35: First, we call the **setUpData()** function and pass the *rRow* variable to it (the data from the current row). That function will return the report data we need to then create the report. See script 2 for more details.

L37-38: Then we call the **createReport()** function and pass the company name, the template document, the report folder the current row data, and the report data. This will return the made report. See script 3 for more details.

L40-41: We then call the **addToSheet()** function to add the link to the sheet and update the make report column. This will return the fact that the report has been made. See script 4 for more details.

L43: This loops around for each report and then we close the *reportRows* **forEach()** loop.

At the end we will inform the user whether any reports have been made or not with a simple toast message.

```
45.        //End of script message to user
46.        if (reportMade === true) {
47.          ss.toast("Reports made.");
48.        } else {
49.          ss.toast("No reports made.")
50.        }
51.      }
```

L46-47: We check if the variable *reportMade* is true, if so, it shows the "Reports made" message.

L48-51: If none have been made, it'll show the "No reports made" message.

Script 2

To set up all the data ready for the report.

```
1. function setUpData(rRow) {
2.
3.   let [rGroup, rLang, rClassLevel, rTeacher, rStudent,
4.       rEmail, rPeriod, rSpeaking, rListening, rWriting,
5.       rReading, rGrammar, rVocab, rExam, rAttendance,
6.       rStudentLevel, rLevelProg] = rRow;
```

L1: We open the function and pass the row data, *rRow*.

L2-6: We unpack the contents of the rRow and assign the elements to variables, called **destructuring** an array.

Next, I need to set up more variables which will be used later.

```
8.       const notEval = "Not evaluated";
9.       let textS = "X", textL = "X", textW = "X",
10.          textR = "X", textG = "X", textV = "X";
11.      let speakCol, listCol, writCol, readCol, gramCol, vocaCol;
```

L8: If there isn't a mark for any of the criteria, I want to add a "Not evaluated" message. I've stored it in a variable here, as if I want to change that message in the future, I only have to change it here and not in every place in the code.

L9-10: I then set the default values for the criteria, which will be an X at the end of each row, to show the grade for that row.

L11: I also set up the variables to store the column numbers for each of the criteria grades. They need to be declared here, so that they are visible later in the code.

Next, I want to deal with the group number and if the number is less than 10, I want it to be prefixed with a zero.

```
13.      //Add group number - deal with
14.      let group;
15.      if (!isNaN(rGroup)) {
16.        group = (rGroup > 9) ? rGroup : "0" + rGroup;
17.      }
```

L14: Set up the variable *group* to store the new group value.

L15: Then we need to check that the value we have is a number. To do so, we can use a double negative. We can say if it isn't not a number (NaN) then run the next line of code. So, it will run line 16 if *group* is a number.

L16: Here we'll use a ternary operator to do one of two things. We check if the group number is larger than 9, if it is we just use the group number, or if it isn't, then we add a zero to the front of it.

The next sections get the marks out of 10 for speaking, etc and work out the column number on the tables we're going to use to display the progress bars. If they aren't numbers, then they add the "Not evaluated" text in the first column.

I'm going to go through an example with the speaking mark to explain what's happening. Then we'll see how we can reduce the amount of code by making this generic for all the criteria marks.

```
EXAMPLE
//Get the column numbers & cell values for the marks
if (isNaN(rSpeaking)) {
   speakCol = 1;
   textS = notEval;
} else {
   speakCol = Math.ceil(rSpeaking / 2);
}
```

First, we check to see if the speaking value is NOT a number.

If it is, we set the *speaking* variable as 1. This will be used to set the column number for speaking.

The text we add in the cell will be "Not evaluated".

If it is a number, we get the speaking mark and divide it by 2. So, a mark of 10 will leave 5, and a mark of 9 will leave 4.5. What we need is a whole number to use as a column number, so the odd numbers we'll need to round up to the nearest number. We do that by using **Math.ceil(number)**. So, a mark of 9 will produce a column number of 5.

We could then repeat that code for the other marks, but we can do it in much less code. First, we need to set up the variables we're going to use in arrays. The order of the arrays is important, so that each of the criteria are in the same position.

For example, the speaking mark, the speaking column, and the speaking text are all in position 0.

```
19.      const marks = [rSpeaking, rListening, rWriting,
20.               rReading, rGrammar, rVocab];
21.      const critCols = [speakCol, listCol, writCol,
22.               readCol, gramCol,  vocaCol];
```

```
23.          const texts = [textS, textL, textW, textR, textG, textV];
```

L19-20: This array contains the marks.

L21-22: This contains the column numbers we'll calculate.

L23: This holds the text that will go in the rows.

Now, we set up our generic **forEach** to get the column numbers and to determine what text is added.

```
25.        //Get the column numbers & cell values for the marks
26.        marks.forEach((mark, ind) => {
27.          if (isNaN(mark)) {
28.            critCols[ind] = 1;
29.            texts[ind] = notEval;
30.          } else {
31.            critCols[ind] = Math.ceil(mark / 2);
32.          }
33.        });
```

L26: Iterate through the *marks* array. Use *ind* to track the current index number.

L27: Check to see if the current mark is not a number.

L28: If it isn't, add 1 to the criteria column, using the index to assign it to the correct one in the array.

L29: Similarly, we add the 'Not evaluated' text to the text at position *ind*.

L30-33: If the mark is a number, we divide by 2, round it up if necessary and add it to the *critCols* variable at position *ind*.

```
35.        //Set the exam mark format and attendance
36.        if (!isNaN(rExam)) {
37.          rExam = rExam + " / 10";
38.        }
39.
40.        attendance = (rAttendance * 100).toFixed(0);
```

L36: Check if the exam mark is a number by checking if it isn't not a number. You could also add a check to see if it's between 0 and 10.

L37: Add out of 10 to the exam mark. If it isn't a number, it will just use that value. For example, a teacher might write 'No exam'.

L40: Get the attendance figure and times by 100 to get the percentage. Change the format of the attendance figure so there are no decimals.

```
41.        //Store the above variables in an array
42.        const reportData = [critCols, texts, group, rExam, attendance,
43.          notEval, rLang, rTeacher, rStudent, rPeriod,
44.          rStudentLevel, rLevelProg];
45.        return reportData;
46.      }
```

L42-44: Store all the variables we need in the next part in an array called *reportData*.

L45: Return that array back to line 35 in script 1.

The **createReport()** function is then called.

Script 3
Create the report

This is the script that will create the report and is called from line 37 in script 1. It's divided up into lots of functions, each creating a specific part of the report.

```
1.  function createReport(company, reportTemplate, reportFolder, reportData) {
2.
3.      //Destructure the reportData array
4.      [critCols, texts, group, rExam, attendance, notEval,
5.      rLang, rTeacher, rStudent, rPeriod,
6.      rStudentLevel, rLevelProg] = reportData;
```

L1: Open the function and pass the company name, the report template, the report folder, and the report data from the last script.

L3-6: Destructure the *reportData* array and assign the variables. To do this I just copied the array in lines 42-44 in the script 2, as they will match.

Now, let's make a copy of the report template and get it ready to be edited.

```
8.      /Copy template document & name document, get the doc body
9.      const newReport = reportTemplate.makeCopy(company +
10.       "-Report-" + group + "-" + rStudent, reportFolder);
11.      const newReportId = newReport.getId();
12.      const report = DocumentApp.openById(newReportId);
13.      const body = report.getBody();
```

```
14.     const bgColor1 = "#FFB74D", bgColor2 = '#eba845',
15.          bgColor3 = '#fce5cd';
```

L9-10: Make a copy of the report template and name it with the company name, "-Report-" the group number, and the student's name. Then we add it to the report folder.

L11-12: We get the new report's ID and then open it by its ID.

L13: We get its body.

L14-15: We set up the background colours we're going to use, using the hexadecimal codes.

In the report, there are 10 tables (0-9) and these are what we need to edit.

```
17.     //Fill in tables
18.     const tables = body.getTables();
19.     table0(tables, company, rStudent, rPeriod, rTeacher, rLang, group);
20.     tables2to7(tables, bgColor1, bgColor2, bgColor3, reportData);
21.     table8(tables, bgColor1, rStudentLevel, rLevelProg);
22.     table9(tables, rExam, attendance);
```

L18: First, we get all the tables in the body.

L19-22: There are 4 functions we're going to call: the first table, the main marks tables, the level progression one, and the exam mark and attendance one. For each one, we pass the variables we need. We'll look at those in detail later.

```
24.          //save edits and update report made status
25.          report.saveAndClose();
26.          return report;
27.     }
```

L25: Save and close the document.

L26: We return the report back to line 37 in script 1.

Function table0()

```
29.          //Fill in student and group details
30.          function table0(tables, company, rStudent, rPeriod,
31.            rTeacher, rLang, group) {
32.            const table0 = tables[0];
33.            table0.getRow(0).getCell(1).setText(rStudent);
34.            table0.getRow(1).getCell(1).setText(company);
35.            table0.getRow(2).getCell(1).setText(rPeriod);
```

```
36.         table0.getRow(0).getCell(3).setText(rTeacher);
37.         table0.getRow(1).getCell(3).setText(rLang);
38.         table0.getRow(2).getCell(3).setText(group);
39.      }
```

L30: Open the function and pass the tables, the company name, and certain report data variables as parameters.

L31: We get the first table, table0.

L33-38: Now, we add those values to the table. We get the table, get the row number, get the cell number, then use **setText()** to add the value to the cell.

Function tables 2to7()

```
41.         //Fill in feedback and colour cells
42.         function tables2to7(tables, bgColor1, bgColor2, bgColor3,
43.                             reportData) {
44.
45.           const table2 = tables[2], table3 = tables[3],
46.                 table4 = tables[4], table5 = tables[5],
47.                 table6 = tables[6], table7 = tables[7];
```

L42-43: Open the function and pass tables, the background colours, and the report data as parameters.

L45-47: We get the six tables we're going to be editing (from Speaking to Vocabulary).

```
49.         //Destructure reportData array
50.         [critCols, texts, group, rExam, attendance, notEval,
51.         rLang, rTeacher, rStudent, rPeriod,
52.         rStudentLevel, rLevelProg] = reportData;
```

L50-52: Destructure the *reportData* array.

Next, we either add an X in the appropriate column number, or we add "Not evaluated" in column 1.

For the level	Insufficient	OK	Good	Very Good	Excellent
Speaking:			X		

Writing:	Not evaluated				

Similar to what we saw in the last script, we could write code for each table but we can also write a generic one here to add the X or 'Not evaluated' text for each mark.

First, we need three arrays, which contain the 3 sets of variables we need: the first two we already have from the *reportData*, *critCols* (column numbers), *texts* (X or Not evaluated), and we need an array of the tables we're going to edit.

```
49.      //Set up arrays for text, scores out of 5, criteria tables
50.      const tb = [table2, table3, table4, table5, table6, table7];
```

L50: Set up the array of tables.

Then we iterate through the tables to then add the background colours and texts.

```
57.      //Adds either "Not evaluated" or X to appropriate column for each table
58.      tb.forEach((table, t) => {
59.
60.        if (texts[t] === notEval) {
61.          table.getRow(0).getCell(1)
62.              .setBackgroundColor(bgColor3).setText(notEval);
63.        }
```

L58: Use **forEach** to iterate through the tables. We'll use *t* as the index to get the data from the other arrays.

L60: Check to see if the current text is 'Not evaluated'.

L61-63: If the value is 'Not evaluated' then it gets the current table, gets the first row, gets the second cell and adds the third background colour (a light orange), and adds the 'Not evaluated' text.

```
64.        else {
65.          for (x = 1; x < critCols[t]; x++) {
66.            table.getRow(0).getCell(x)
67.                .setBackgroundColor(bgColor1);
68.          }
69.          table.getRow(0).getCell(critCols[t])
70.              .setBackgroundColor(bgColor2).setText(texts[t]);
71.        }
72.      });
73.    }
```

L64-65: If the current value is a number, it loops through the cell numbers until it gets to one number before the value in the current criteria column (*critCols[t]*).

L66-68: As it loops through it will add the first background colour (a mid-orange) to the cells up until the cell before where the X will be added.

L69-70: The last cell has a different colour and has the X added to it. So, we get that last cell using the value in the current criteria column, then add the second background colour and add the X (stored in *texts[t]*).

This will update the six criteria tables with the marks and colours.

Function table8()

Here, we're going to add the student's level and their progress within that level.

```
75.    //Fill in level and level progress
76.    function table8(tables, bgColor1, rStudentLevel, rLevelProg) {
77.       const table8 = tables[8];
78.       table8.getRow(0).getCell(1).setText(rStudentLevel);
79.
80.       for (lp = 1; lp <= rLevelProg; lp++) {
81.          table8.getRow(1).getCell(lp)
82.             .setText(">")
83.             .setBackgroundColor(bgColor1);
84.       }
85.    }
```

L76-77: Open the function and pass the tables, first background colour, student's level, and student's level progression. Then get table 8.

L78: In the first row, second cell, we add the student's level.

L80: Similar to above, here we loop through the cells until we get to the level progress value.

L81-83: Each loop we get the second row, get the current cell, add the ">" symbol and set the background colour.

L84-85: We close the loop and function.

Function table9()

Finally, we're going to add the exam mark and the attendance figure in the last table.

```
87.    //Fill in exam & attendance info
88.    function table9(tables, rExam, attendance) {
89.       const table9 = tables[9];
90.       table9.getRow(0).getCell(1).setText(rExam);
```

```
91.    table9.getRow(0).getCell(3).setText(attendance + "%");
92. }
```

L88: Open the function and pass the table, exam mark, and attendance.

L89: Get the last table.

L90-91: Add the exam mark to the second cell and the attendance figure with a percent symbol, to the fourth cell.

Script 4

The final part is to update the Google Sheet with the document link, change the report status to "Made", and update the progress message to the user.

This is called from line 40 in script 1.

```
1.    function addToSheet(openReport, num, ss, sheet,
2.      numOfReports, rowNo) {
3.      //Add Google Doc URL to Sheet
4.      const reportUrl = openReport.getUrl();
5.      const linkCell = sheet.getRange(rowNo, 23);
6.      linkCell.setFormula('=HYPERLINK("'
7.        + reportUrl
8.        + '";"REPORT")');
9.      sheet.getRange(rowNo, 24).setValue("Made");
```

L1-2: Open the function and pass the report, the current report number being made, the spreadsheet, the sheet, the total number of reports, and the row number of the report.

L4: Get the report URL.

L5: Get the cell we need to add the link to.

L6-8: Now use **setFormula()** to add the hyperlink to the sheet. Here, we use the HYPERLINK function, use the report URL and the text we're going to show is REPORT.

L9: Next to that column we need to change the 'Make' column from "Y" to "Made".

The final thing to do is to let the user know which report we've just made and to update the *reportMade* status to true, as we have made a report.

```
11.      //Progress message to user & update reportMade status
12.      const reportNumber = Number(num) + 1;
13.      ss.toast("Report " + reportNumber + " out of "
```

```
14.            + numOfReports + " made.");
15.         reportMade = true;
16.         return reportMade;
17.      }
```

L12: To get the report number, we get the report index from the **forEach()** loop in script 1, stored in the variable *num* and then add 1 as it's zero-based. We need to make *num* a number to be able to do the addition.

L13-14: Then display the toast message with the current report number out of the total number of reports.

L15-16: Set the *reportMade* status to true. Then return the *reportMade* status to L40 in script 1.

Script 5

The final script is to add a menu to run the program from.

```
1.    function onOpen() {
2.       const ui = SpreadsheetApp.getUi();
3.       ui.createMenu('REPORTS')
4.          .addItem('Make reports', 'makeReports')
5.          .addToUi();
6.    }
```

L1-6: Open the function and get the spreadsheet UI. We create the menu, add the menu item and add it to the UI. Let's add an example and run the program.

In row 5, I've added the student Ringo Sta along with his marks, etc.

Widgets Ltd

Group	Language	Class Level	Teacher	Students	Email	Period
02	English	A2	Mercedes Profesora	Ringo Sta	email3@email.com	oct22-jun23

Speaking	Listening	Writing	Reading	Grammar	Vocabulary
4	4	X	6	4	6

Exam Mark	Attendance	Student Level	P	Progression				Links	Make
5.5	50%	A2	2	X	X			REPORT	Made

77

In column X we select "Y". Then from the REPORTS menu we select "Make Reports".

REPORTS
Make reports

This makes the report and stores it in the folder.

 Widgets Ltd-Report-02-Ringo Sta

Opening the report, we can see it's converted all the data from the sheet into the document. The beauty of this is that you can create multiple documents at the same time.

ENGLISH ACADEMY

PROGRESS REPORT

Name:	Ringo Sta	Teacher:	Mercedes Profesora
Company:	Widgets Ltd	Language:	English
Period:	oct22-jun23	Group:	02

For the level	Insufficient	OK	Good	Very Good	Excellent
Speaking:		X			
Listening:		X			
Writing:	Not evaluated				
Reading:			X		
Grammar:		X			
Vocabulary:			X		

Overall Level:	A2				
Progression:	>	>			

Exam Mark:	5.5 / 10	Attendance:	50%

BARRIE ROBERTS
Director of Studies

7: Emailing reports as a PDF or as a link

In this chapter, we're going to expand the functionality of the program we looked at in the previous chapter. It was great to produce the individual reports, but wouldn't it be even better if we could email them directly to the students?

That's what we're going to look at here. We will look at two options: 1) Email the report as a PDF attachment, or 2) as a link to the Google Doc which when clicked will download as a PDF.

Overview

1) Once the report has been made, the teacher will select the reports they want to send.
2) Then from the menu, they will select the option to send them.
3) This will email the report to the student as a PDF, or as a link to the Google Doc.

Key learning points

1) How to get document URLs from the sheet and convert them into file IDs.
2) How to create PDFs on the fly, by first creating a Google Doc.
3) How to email links and attachments.
4) How to format an email using a HTML file.
5) How to highlight on the sheet, any rows that have not been sent.

First, let's look at the sheet and the data we'll be entering and using.

Sheet

	A	B	C	D	E	F	G
1	**Widgets Ltd**						
2	Group	Language	Class Level	Teacher	Students	Email	Period
3	01	English	A1	Ian Teacher	John Len	baz@bazroberts.com	oct22-jun23
4	01	English	A1	Ian Teacher	Paul Mac	baz@bazroberts.com	oct22-jun23
5	02	English	A2	Mercedes Profesora	Ringo Sta	baz@bazroberts.com	oct22-jun23
6	02	English	A2	Mercedes Profesora	George Har	baz@bazroberts.com	oct22-jun23

	H	I	J	K	L	M	N
	Speaking	Listening	Writing	Reading	Grammar	Vocabulary	Exam Mark
	6	6	8	8	6	6	6.8
	10	6	8	8	8	10	9.2
	4	4	X	6	4	6	5.5
	8	8	8	6	6	10	7.5

O	P	Q	R	S	T	U	V	W	X	Y
Attendance	Student Level	P	Progression					Links	Make	Send
50%	A1	3	X	X	X			REPORT	Made ▾	Y ▾
75%	A2	2	X	X				REPORT	Made ▾	Y ▾
50%	A2	2	X	X					N ▾	N ▾
90%	A2	4	X	X	X	X			N ▾	N ▾

Email

There will be 2 types of email that can be sent.

The first will contain a link which will allow the student to download the report as a PDF.

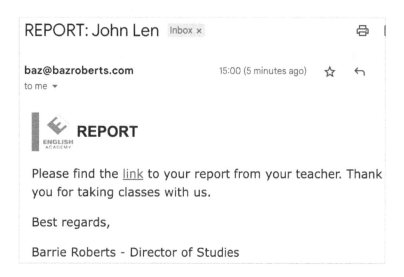

The second will attach the report as a PDF in the email.

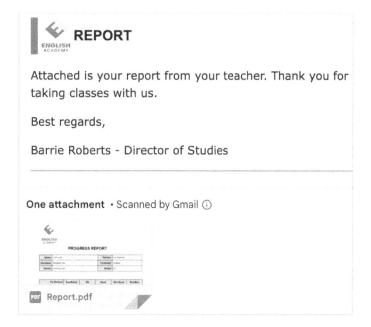

The code to create the reports is the same as what we saw in chapter 6. So, let's look at the code to email the reports.

The code

For this there are 4 script files and 1 HTML file:

5-sendReports – This is the main script to send the reports. It has a function for sending the reports as a PDF (**sendReportsPDF()**), and one to send them as a link (**sendReportsLINK()**). This then calls the main function **sendReports()**.

6a-sendEmailPDF – This emails the reports as PDF attachments.

6b-sendEmailLINK – This sends emails with a link to the reports.

7-email – This is the HTML file to style the email for sending the reports.

8-onOpen – This sets up the menu to run the scripts from.

Script 5
Main script to send reports

```
1. function sendReportsLINK() {
2.    const emailType = 'LINK';
3.    sendReports(emailType);
4. }
5.
6. function sendReportsPDF() {
7.    const emailType = 'PDF';
8.    sendReports(emailType);
9. }
```

L1: If the send reports as links option is chosen, this function will be called. Open the **sendReportsLINK()** function.

L2: Set the email type as "LINK".

L3: Call the **sendReports()** function and pass the email type.

L6: If the send reports as PDFs option is chosen, this function will be called. Open the **sendReportsPDF()** function.

L7: Set the email type as "PDF".

L8: Call the **sendReports()** function and pass the email type.

```
11. function sendReports(emailType) {
12.     //Get data
13.     const ss = SpreadsheetApp.getActiveSpreadsheet();
14.     const sheet = ss.getActiveSheet();
15.     const data = sheet.getDataRange().getValues();
16.     data.splice(0, 2);
17.     const dataFormulas = sheet.getDataRange().getFormulas();
18.     dataFormulas.splice(0, 2);
19.     const image = DriveApp.getFileById("IAMGE FILE ID").getBlob();
20.     const studentCol = 4, emailCol = 5, linkCol = 22, sendCol = 24;
21.     let reportSent = false;
```

L11: Open the **sendReports()** function passing the *emailType* parameter in.

L13-16: Get the data from the Google Sheet and remove the first two rows.

L17-18: Get all the formulas on the sheet. We'll use this to get the report links. Again remove the first two rows.

L19: Get the blob of the academy logo image. Add your image file ID here.

L20: Set the column numbers reference, where some of the data is.

L21: Start with the report sent as false. This will track if reports have been sent.

```
23.     //Filter rows by reports with "Y" in Send column
24.     const reportRows = data.map((rr, index) => {
25.         rr.push(index);
26.         return rr;
27.     })
28.     .filter((rr) => {
29.         return rr[sendCol] === "Y";
30.     });
```

We want to filter the data from the sheet so we only have the rows that have the Sent column marked with a "Y". This is the same way we did it in the last chapter.

L24: We use **map()** to loop through data and each row will be in rr.

L25: We also need to get the row index to get the row number later, so we push that into the array.

L26-27: We then return *rr* into the array *reportRows*.

L28-30: We then filter the rows and only store the ones that have the Send column marked with a "Y".

We now iterate through the *reportRows* array to get the data ready to email and to send either an email with a PDF or a link.

```
32.    reportRows.forEach((rRow) => {
33.      //Get current row index and row
34.      const rowIndex = rRow[25];
35.      const rowNo = rowIndex + 3;
36.      const sEmail = rRow[emailCol];
```

L32: Iterate through reportRows.

L34-35: Get the row index and then work out the row number on the sheet.

L36: Get the student's email address.

Next we check if there is an email address and if so, we get the report formula, extract the ID, then get the document using that ID. We'll also get the student's name.

```
38.        //If there's an email, get the report link and doc
39.        if (sEmail !== "") {
40.          const linkFormula = dataFormulas[rowIndex][linkCol];
41.          let linkId =
      linkFormula.replace('=HYPERLINK("https://docs.google.com/a/bazroberts.com/op
      en?id=', "");
42.          linkId = linkId.replace('","REPORT")', "");
43.          const doc = DriveApp.getFileById(linkId);
44.          const studentName = rRow[studentCol];
```

L39: Check if there is an email. Here, I'm just checking if it's blank or not.

L40: Get the link formula on the current row from the *dataFormulas* array.

```
=HYPERLINK("https://docs.google.com/open?id=1mrcqAqBDHdfli4bMyFFtj6hwW-
vO54LOpD_fuxcMYg","REPORT")
```

L41: Remove the first part of the formula by replacing the HYPERLINK part with nothing. Note, your link will look a bit different from this, as I'm using my Workspace business account and so, it contains my business name. Just replace this with what is on your sheet.

L42: Remove the part after the ID.

L43: Get the document using the file ID you've just extracted.

L44: Get the student's name from the row data.

Next, we call the function that will send the email with a PDF attachment or the function which will send it as a link.

```
46.     //Send report either as a PDF or via a link
47.     if (emailType === "PDF") {
48.       sendEmailPDF(sEmail, studentName, doc, image);
49.     }
50.     else if (emailType === "LINK") {
51.       sendEmailLINK(sEmail, studentName, doc, image, linkId);
52.     }
53.   }
```

L47-49: If the email type is a PDF, then run the **sendEmailPDF()** function and pass the student's email, their name, the report document, and the logo image as parameters.

L50-53: If the email type is a link, then run the **sendEmailLINK()** function and pass the same parameters plus the file ID.

We'll look at those functions in detail later.

```
55.     //If email is missing change cell to red
56.     else {
57.       sheet.getRange(rowNo, 6).setBackground("red");
58.     }
```

L56: We run the following code if the email cell is blank.

L57: We then get the email cell and set the background colour to red.

Once the report is sent, we need to let the user know it was sent ok on the sheet.

```
60.     //Update sheet with "Sent"
61.     sheet.getRange(rowNo, sendCol + 1).setValue("Sent");
62.     reportSent = true;
63.   });
```

L61: Update the Send status on the sheet to "Sent".

L62: Update the *reportSent* variable to true, as we have sent a report.

The final part is to display a message to the user if reports have been sent or not.

```
65.    //End of script msg to user
66.    if (reportSent === true) {
67.      ss.toast("Reports sent.");
68.    } else {
69.      ss.toast("No reports sent.")
70.    }
71. }
```

L66: We check if the *reportSent* variable is true.

L67: If so, we display the toast message "Reports sent.".

L68-71: If not it displays "No reports sent.".

Script 6a
This function will send an email with a link to download the report as a PDF.

```
1. function sendEmailLINK(sEmail, studentName, doc, image, linkId) {
2.   let emailBody = HtmlService.createHtmlOutputFromFile('7-email')
3.                              .getContent();
```

L1: Open the function and pass the parameters, student's email and name, the report, logo image, and the report file ID.

L2-3: Here, we use the **HtmlService** to create the email format from the HTML template we've stored in the HTML script file "7-email". We use the **createHtmlOutputFromFile()** method and then get its content. We store this in the *emailBody* variable.

```
5.    //Change doc access to anyone with link and view permission
6.    doc.setSharing(DriveApp.Access.ANYONE_WITH_LINK,
7.      DriveApp.Permission.VIEW);
```

L6-7: We make sure that the person receiving the email can access the file, by setting the file sharing. To do so, we use the **setSharing()** method and set the access to "anyone with a link" and the permission to "VIEW".

```
9.        //Create URL for the link & add to email
10.       const linkUrl = "https://docs.google.com/document/d/"
11.         + linkId + "/export?format=pdf";
12.       const firstSent = "<p>Please find the <a href=#LINK>link</a> to your
     report from your teacher. Thank you for taking classes with us.</p >";
```

L10-11: We create the download link by adding the ...docs.google.com... part to the file ID and the suffix: **/export?format=pdf**

This will download the file as a PDF. If we just wanted to give them access to the Google Doc, we could just add the suffix "/preview", which will just show the document without being able to edit it.

L12: I've used just one HTML file in this example, but the first sentence is different between the PDF email and the link email. So, we can add a placeholder in the HTML and then replace it with the code we want.

For the link email, I've added a paragraph which includes a placeholder for the link. The `<a href=#LINK>link</a>` part will add the link to the text "link".

```
14.        //Replace the two placeholders in the HTML
15.        emailBody = emailBody.replace('#FIRSTSENT', firstSent);
16.        emailBody = emailBody.replace('#LINK', linkUrl);
```

L15: Replace the placeholder in the HTML "#FIRSTSENT" with the HTML we added above.

L16: Replace the link placeholder in that HTML with the link URL.

```
14.        MailApp.sendEmail(sEmail, "REPORT: " + studentName, '',
15.        {
16.          htmlBody: emailBody,
17.          inlineImages: { logo: image },
18.          replyTo: 'baz@bazroberts.com'
19.        });
20.        }
```

L14: We use **MailApp** and **sendEmail()** to send the email and pass the student's email and the title of the email, i.e. "REPORT: " + the student's name. The next parameter we leave blank, as we're using a HTML email.

L15: We can set some options to the email.

L16: Being a HTML email, we need to use the **htmlBody** option and pass the *emailBody* variable we created above.

L17: I want the academy logo at the top of the email, so we use the *inlineImages* options to add that and pass the *image* variable.

L18: I also want the student to be able to reply back to my email address. I add this as sometimes I use a different email address to send the emails out. To do this we use the **replyTo** option and add the email address we want them to reply back to.

L19-20: Close the options and function.

Script 6b

Let's now look at the other email option, which sends the report as a PDF attachment.

```
1. function sendEmailPDF(sEmail, studentName, doc, image) {
2.    let emailBody = HtmlService.createHtmlOutputFromFile('7-email')
3.    .getContent();
```

L1: Open the function and pass the student's email and name, and the report.

L2-3: Use the **HtmlService** to create the email body from the "7-email" file.

```
5.    //Get G Doc and make a PDF then attach
6.    const pdf = doc.getAs('application/pdf').getBytes();
7.    const attach = {
8.        fileName: 'Report.pdf', content: pdf,
9.        mimeType: 'application/pdf'
10.       };
```

L6: Get the Google Doc report and convert it into a PDF by getting it as a PDF and getting the bytes of the file, then storing that in the variable *pdf*.

To make an attachment, you need the file name, the file, and the file type.

L7-8: Here we store the 3 pieces of information in an object by using the curly brackets. All this is stored in the *attach* variable.

```
11.        const firstSent = "<p>Attached is your report from your teacher. Thank
      you for taking classes with us.</p>"
12.        emailBody = emailBody.replace('#FIRSTSENT', firstSent);
```

L11: As we did in the email above, we set up a HTML line for the first sentence. This time it's just text in between the <p> tags.

L12: We then replace the #FIRSTSENT placeholder with this text.

```
14.        MailApp.sendEmail(sEmail, "REPORT: " + studentName, '',
15.        {
16.        htmlBody: emailBody,
17.        inlineImages: { logo: image },
18.        replyTo: 'baz@bazroberts.com',
19.        attachments: [attach]
```

```
20.          });
21.      }
```

L14-21: This is basically the same as we did in the other email, except that in line 19, we add the option for attachments and pass the *attach* variable containing the PDF document.

HTML 7

This HTML file is the email template. This is what we are aiming to achieve:

REPORT: John Len   Inbox ×

baz@bazroberts.com
to me ▾

 **REPORT**

Please find the link to your report from your teacher. Thank you for taking classes with us.

Best regards,

Barrie Roberts - Director of Studies

```
1.  <!DOCTYPE html>
2.  <html>
3.
4.  <head>
5.     <base target="_top">
```

L1: We state it's a HTML document.

L2 and 4: We open the html and head tags.

L5: Set the default action of clicking on a link. Here, it will open a new page when they click on the link.

```
6.     <style>
7.       p {
8.        font-family: verdana;
9.        font-size: 1.2em;
10.       }
```

L6: We open the style tag.

L7: Using CSS we set the paragraph styling using the p tag.

L8-9: We set the font to Verdana and the font size to 1.2 em.

```
12.          #image {
13.              float: left;
14.              width: 50px;
15.              height: 50px;
16.              padding-left: 10px;
17.          }
```

L12-17: Now we set the ID "image" styling. We place the image to the left using float, set its width and height, and give it a little bit of padding on the left.

```
19.          #title {
20.              height: 40px;
21.              padding-top: 10px;
22.              border-left-style: outset;
23.              border-left-color: red;
24.              border-left-width: 10px;
25.          }
```

L19-25: Here, we set the styling for the title in the email. We set its height, and a bit of padding to the top of it. Then I want to add a small red rectangle on the left, so we can use border-left and the outset style (i.e. a normal filled rectangle), colour it red and set its width.

```
27.          .pad {
28.              padding-left: 10px;
29.          }
30.      </style>
31.  </head>
```

L27-29: Here, we add some padding to the class "pad".
L30-31: Close the style and head tags.

Now we've set up the styling, we need to add the main body of email.

```
33.  <body>
34.      <div class="pad">
35.          <img id="image" src=cid:logo>
36.          <h2 id="title">REPORT</h2>
37.          #FIRSTSENT
38.          <p>Best regards,</p>
39.          <p>Barrie Roberts - Director of Studies</p>
40.          <hr>
```

```
41.         </div>
42.        </body>
43.
44.        </html>
```

L33: Open the body tag.

L34: Open a div and add the class "pad" to add the padding.

L35-36: Add the logo image, styling it with the ID "image" and the link is stored in the logo property we sent up in script 6a and 6b. Note, the file has to be shared with anyone, otherwise, they won't see it in the email. So, make sure that's set up on the file in your Drive.

L36: Add a title using a <h2> tag and style it with ID "title" which will also add the red rectangle to the left.

L37: Add the first sentence placeholder, which will be replaced by the sentence we set up earlier.

L38-40: Add the rest of the text and a horizontal rule.

L41-44: We close the div, the body, and html tags.

Script 8
Create menu to run programs

In this final script, we'll create the menu from which we'll be able to run the programs form.

```
REPORTS

 Make reports


 Send reports as PDF attachment


 Send reports as link
```

```
1.  function onOpen() {
2.    const ui = SpreadsheetApp.getUi();
3.    ui.createMenu('REPORTS')
4.       .addItem('Make reports', 'makeReports')
5.       .addSeparator()
6.       .addItem('Send reports as PDF attachment', 'sendReportsPDF')
7.       .addSeparator()
8.       .addItem('Send reports as link', 'sendReportsLINK')
9.       .addToUi();
```

90

```
10.          }
```

L1-3: Open the function **onOpen()**. Get the spreadsheet UI, create the menu and call it "REPORTS".

L4-8: Add the menu items and their associated functions. I've added a separator in between them to add a dividing line between the options.

L9: Add all this to the UI.

Ok, let's send a report. The report's already been made, so we just select Y in the Send column.

Links	Make	Send		Links	Make	Send
REPORT	Made ▾	Sent ▾		REPORT	Made ▾	Sent ▾
REPORT	Made ▾	Y ▾		REPORT	Made ▾	Sent ▾

We then select one of the send options from the REPORTS menu. Once the report has been sent, it updates the Send column to "Sent".

The student receives the email with the report attached as a PDF.

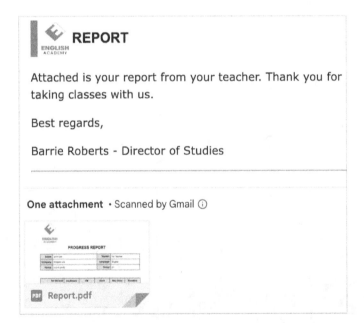

8: Create multiple reports in one document

In this chapter, we're going to look at how we can create multiple-page documents. As an example, we're going to create a document which contains several certificates which can then be printed out from one file, rather than having to open individual files.

At our academy in the past, we had two different certificates, which were pre-printed with whether the students had passed or not and the problem was that we had to order two different types of certificates and sometimes even have to print out both types as we didn't know if a student had passed until the last minute.

With this code, we now only need one type of certificate paper and we create one document which contains the two types in it, reducing our costs, and making the process quicker.

Overview

1) We enter the students' details on the Google Sheet.
2) We then enter the row numbers we want to make.
3) We run the program from the menu and it makes one multi-page document which contains all the certificates.
4) It then adds a link to the document on the sheet.

Key learning points

1) How to append cells to tables with arrays.
2) How to set cell widths and attributes.
3) How to set table cell border colours.
4) How to add page breaks to create multi-page documents.

First, let's look at the sheet and the data we'll be entering and using.

Sheet

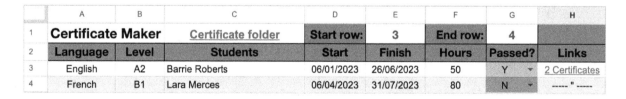

	A	B	C	D	E	F	G	H
1	**Certificate Maker**		Certificate folder	Start row:	3	End row:	4	
2	Language	Level	Students	Start	Finish	Hours	Passed?	Links
3	English	A2	Barrie Roberts	06/01/2023	26/06/2023	50	Y	2 Certificates
4	French	B1	Lara Merces	06/04/2023	31/07/2023	80	N	----- " -----

We enter the language they studied, the level, their name, the course start and finish dates, the number of hours they studied and whether they passed or not. Then a link to the document containing the certificates will be added.

Printed certificate

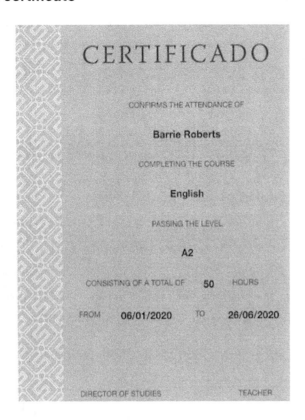

The code

There are 5 script files in this project:

1-Main script to make certificates

2-The styling is stored in its own file

3-Add the data to the document

4-Update the sheet and move the file

5-Create the menu to run the program when the spreadsheet is opened

Script 1
Main script to make certificates

```
1. function makeCerts() {
2.   const ss = SpreadsheetApp.getActiveSpreadsheet(),
3.   shCerts = ss.getSheetByName('CERTIFICATES'),
4.   data = shCerts.getDataRange().getValues();
```

L1-4: Open the function. Get the spreadsheet, then the sheet called CERTIFICATES and get the values on that sheet.

```
6.    //Get start and end row
7.    const startRowNum = data[0][4], endRowNum = data[0][6];
```

L7: We get the start row and end row values from cells E1 and G1.

```
9.        if (endRowNum >= startRowNum) {
10.           //Get today's date
11.           const timeZone = Session.getScriptTimeZone(),
12.           date = new Date(),
13.           fDate = Utilities.formatDate(date, timeZone,
14.             'yyyy-MM-dd HH.mm');
```

L9: We check to see if the end row is greater than or equal to the start row. This is just to check we've entered logical values, i.e. we can't have a start row larger than an end one.

L11-14: We get the time zone and today's date and then format it. We'll use this in the file name for the certificates document.

In this part we'll create the document and get its body.

```
16.          //////MAKE DOC/////
17.          //Get certificate, folder, and certificate body
18.          const newCert = DocumentApp.create("Certificates - " + fDate);
19.          const certFolder = DriveApp.getFolderById('FOLDER ID');
20.          const newCertId = newCert.getId();
21.          const openCert = DocumentApp.openById(newCertId);
22.          const body = openCert.getBody();
```

L18: Here, we create a new document and name it.

L19: We get the folder we want to store the certificates in. Add your folder ID.

L20-21: We get the newly created document's ID and use that to open it.

L22: We then get its body.

Next, we call three separate functions to add the styling, the data, and then to update the Google Sheet.

First, we set up the styling we want to use. I usually store this in a separate script file, to keep the code clean and easy to read.

```
24.        //Get styles
25.        const style = setupStyling();
26.
27.        ////ADD DATA TO DOC////
28.        addData(style, startRowNum, endRowNum, data,
29.          timeZone, body, shCerts, openCert);
30.
31.        ////UPDATE SHEET////
32.        updateSheet(newCertId, certFolder, startRowNum,
33.          endRowNum, shCerts, ss);
```

L25: We call the **setupStyling()** function and return the results to the variable *style*. We'll look at the details in script 2 below.

Next, we need to add the data from our sheet to the document.

L28-29: We call the **addData()** function and pass various parameters to it. We'll look at the details in script 3 below.

Once the certificates are made, we need to add the link to the document to the sheet and also to move the document to the folder we want to store it in.

L32-33: We call the function **updateSheet()** and pass various parameters to it. We'll look at the details in script 4 below.

```
34.        }
35.        else {
36.          Browser.msgBox("Start row entered is larger than end row.");
37.        }
38.      }
```

L34: We close the if statement.

L35-38: If the end row number is larger than the start row, then we display a message in the browser alerting the user.

Script 2
To set up the styles used in the certificates

```
1. function setupStyling() {
2.    //Set up styling
3.    const center = DocumentApp.HorizontalAlignment.CENTER;
4.    const style0 = {}; //Common text
5.    style0[DocumentApp.Attribute.HORIZONTAL_ALIGNMENT] = center;
```

```
6.    style0[DocumentApp.Attribute.FONT_FAMILY] = 'Helvetica Neue';
7.    style0[DocumentApp.Attribute.FONT_SIZE] = 12;
```

L1: Open the function.

L3: First, we add the center horizontal alignment to a variable as we will use this more than once.

L4: We set up a variable to hold the first style as an object. This will be for the common text on the certificate, i.e. not the specific student information.

L5-7: We set up the horizontal alignment to center, the font family to 'Helvetica Neue', the font size to 12.

```
9.        const style1 = {};   //Student text
10.       style1[DocumentApp.Attribute.HORIZONTAL_ALIGNMENT] = center;
11.       style1[DocumentApp.Attribute.FONT_FAMILY] = 'Helvetica Neue';
12.       style1[DocumentApp.Attribute.FONT_SIZE] = 16;
13.       style1[DocumentApp.Attribute.BOLD] = true;
14.
15.       const style = [style0, style1];
16.       return style;
17.    }
```

L9: Now, we set up a style for the student-specific information.

L10-13: The style is similar to before except here the font size is 16 and it is bolded.

L15-17: We then store those styles in an array called *style*, and return that.

Script 3

This script adds the sheet data to the document. First, let's set up the variables for the column references and styles.

```
1. function addData(style, startRowNum, endRowNum, data,
2.    timeZone, body, shCerts, openCert) {
3.
4.    //Column references and styles
5.    const langCol = 0, levCol = 1, stCol = 2, startCol = 3,
6.    finishCol = 4, hrsCol = 5, passedCol = 6, linkCol = 7;
7.    const [s0, s1] = style;
8.    const borderColor = '#FFFFFF';
```

L1-2: Open the function and pass the styles, the row start and end numbers, the sheet data, the time zone, the document body, the certificates sheet and opened document.

L5-6: To make it easier to see where the data is coming from, here we'll set up some variables that relate to the array positions of the data.

L7: Destructure the style array and assign the two styles to two variables.

L8: Set the border colour for the tables we're going to add to white, so that they don't appear.

```
10.              /////LOOP THRU STUDENT DATA/////
11.        const sRowNumbA = startRowNum - 1;
12.        for (let sRow = sRowNumbA; sRow < endRowNum; sRow++) {
13.          //Get student data - Set up variables
14.          const dataRow = data[sRow];
15.          const language = dataRow[langCol];
16.          const studentName = dataRow[stCol];
17.          const sLevel = dataRow[levCol];
18.          const hours = dataRow[hrsCol];
19.          const passed = dataRow[passedCol];
```

L11: Get the start row and subtract 1 to get the array index.

L12: Now the start looping through the data and only between the start and end rows.

L14: As we will be referring to the data and the current row, we put this in a variable to not have to refer to the array position every time.

L15-19: Here, we'll set up variables for the student data we're getting from our sheet.

Next, let's get the course dates and format them.

```
21.        //Format dates
22.        let startDate = dataRow[startCol];
23.        startDate = Utilities.formatDate(startDate, timeZone,
24.          'dd/MM/yyyy');
25.        let finishDate = dataRow[finishCol];
26.          finishDate = Utilities.formatDate(finishDate, timeZone,
27.          'dd/MM/yyyy');
```

L22-27: Get the dates and format them.

Now, we can start adding things to our certificate document.

```
29.        //Add blank lines at the top of the doc
30.        for (let p = 0; p < 7; p++) {
31.          body.appendParagraph('');
32.        }
```

L30-32: First, I want to add some space at the top. A simple way to do that is just to append a number of blank paragraphs. To avoid repetitive lines, here we have a simple for loop to add 7 blank lines.

Next, are the first two lines of text.

```
34.        //Confirms and student name
35.        const t1Cells = [['', 'CONFIRMS THE ATTENDANCE OF']];
36.        const t1 = body.appendTable(t1Cells);
37.        const t2Cells = [['', studentName]];
38.        const t2 = body.appendTable(t2Cells);
```

L35: First, we create the cells we want in our table. In most of the parts below, we're going to have a 1 row table with 2 columns, i.e. 2 cells. We set this up by creating an array of arrays. We have one array with the first cell as blank, as this will be used just to position the text, and the second with the text we want to show.

Then we put that within another array to show it's just 1 row, and we store it in a variable.

L36: We then get the body and append a table using the content of the array we just set up then store it in the variable *t1*.

We'll add some more styling and positioning later.

L37-38: We then do the same for the next table, which will show the student's name.

Next, is the course language info.

```
40.        //Completing and Language
41.        const t3Cells = [['', 'COMPLETING THE COURSE']];
42.        const t3 = body.appendTable(t3Cells);
43.        const t4Cells = [['', language]];
44.        const t4 = body.appendTable(t4Cells);
```

L41-44: Set up the cells for the next two tables and append it to the body.

The next table will show either "passing the level" or just "level" depending on whether they passed the course or not.

```
46.        //Passing & Level
47.        let t5Cells;
48.        if (passed === "Y") {
49.          t5Cells = [['', 'PASSING THE LEVEL']];
50.        }
```

```
51.        else { t5Cells = [['', 'LEVEL']]; }
52.        const t5 = body.appendTable(t5Cells);
53.
54.        const t6Cells = [['', sLevel]];
55.        const t6 = body.appendTable(t6Cells);
```

L47: Set up the variable to hold the text.

L48-50: Check to see if they have passed, if so, add the first text.

L51: If not, add the second text.

L52: Append the table.

L54-55: Set up the next table, which shows the student's level.

Next, let's set the widths of the tables so far. We could have done this as we went along, but as they have the same widths, we can do it with **forEach** and an array.

```
57.        //Set widths of first 6 tables
58.        const widthFromLeft = 180;
59.        const widthToRight = 350;
60.        const firstTables = [t1, t2, t3, t4, t5, t6];
61.        firstTables.forEach((fTable) => {
62.          fTable.getRow(0).getCell(0).setWidth(widthFromLeft);
63.          fTable.getRow(0).getCell(1).setWidth(widthToRight);
64.        });
```

L58: Each of the tables has two cells. The width of the first cell dictates how far to the right the next cell will start from.

L59: Secondly, we set the width of the second cell, which in this case will take it to the edge of the page.

L60: Put the six tables in an array.

L61: Iterate through that array.

L62-64: Apply the width to the first and second cell of each table, then close the **forEach** loop.

The next tables have more cells and the widths will depend on the content in each one. So, we add the widths and styling to each one.

```
66.        //Hours
67.        const t7Cells = [['', 'CONSISTING OF A TOTAL OF',
```

```
68.                          hours.toFixed(0), 'HOURS']];
69.        const t7 = body.appendTable(t7Cells);
70.        t7.getRow(0).getCell(0).setWidth(widthFromLeft);
71.        t7.getRow(0).getCell(1).setWidth(180);
72.        t7.getRow(0).getCell(2).setWidth(60);
73.        t7.getRow(0).getCell(3).setWidth(60);
74.        t7.getCell(0, 2).getChild(0).asParagraph()
75.          .setAttributes(s1);
76.        t7.getCell(0, 3).getChild(0).asParagraph()
77.          .setAttributes(s0);
```

L67-68: Set up the four cells. I've formatted the hours so there aren't any decimal points.

L69: Append the table.

L70-73: Set the widths of the four cells.

L74-77: Set the styling of the third and fourth cells. Note, the second cell will be done in a loop with the other tables later.

```
79.        //Dates
80.        const t8Cells = [['', 'FROM', startDate, 'TO', finishDate]];
81.        const t8 = body.appendTable(t8Cells);
82.        t8.getRow(0).getCell(0).setWidth(widthFromLeft);
83.        t8.getRow(0).getCell(1).setWidth(50);
84.        t8.getRow(0).getCell(2).setWidth(135);
85.        t8.getRow(0).getCell(3).setWidth(40);
86.        t8.getRow(0).getCell(4).setWidth(135);
87.        t8.getCell(0, 2).getChild(0).asParagraph()
88.          .setAttributes(s1);
89.        t8.getCell(0, 3).getChild(0).asParagraph()
90.          .setAttributes(s0);
91.        t8.getCell(0, 4).getChild(0).asParagraph()
92.          .setAttributes(s1);
```

L80-81: Set the content of the 5 cells and append the table.

L82-86: Set the cell widths.

L87-92: Set the styling to the third, fourth, and fifth cells. Again, the second cell will be done later.

Next, let's add a gap before the next table.

```
94.        for (p = 0; p < 5; p++) {
95.            body.appendParagraph('');
96.        }
```

L94-96: As we did earlier, we can use a loop to add a few empty lines.

Then we add the final table.

```
98.        //Signatures
99.        const t9Cells = [['', 'DIRECTOR OF STUDIES', '', 'TEACHER']];
100.       const t9 = body.appendTable(t9Cells);
101.       t9.getRow(0).getCell(0).setWidth(widthFromLeft);
102.       t9.getRow(0).getCell(1).setWidth(150);
103.       t9.getRow(0).getCell(2).setWidth(70);
104.       t9.getRow(0).getCell(3).setWidth(150);
105.       t9.getCell(0, 2).getChild(0).asParagraph()
106.          .setAttributes(s0);
107.       t9.getCell(0, 3).getChild(0).asParagraph()
108.          .setAttributes(s0);
```

L99-100: Set up the four cells and append the table.

L101-104: Set the widths of the four cells.

L105-108: Set the styling of the third and fourth cells. Note, the second cell will be done in a loop with the other tables later.

Now, we can add some additional styling to multiple tables. First of all, let's change the default black border of the tables to white, so they aren't shown.

```
110.       //Change border colour on all tables
111.       const tables = [t1, t2, t3, t4, t5, t6, t7, t8, t9];
112.       tables.forEach((table) => {
113.          table.setBorderColor(borderColor);
114.       });
```

L111: Add all the tables in an array.

L112-114: Iterate through them and set the border colour to white.

Now, let's add the style, *s0*, to some of the tables.

```
116.        //Add styling
117.        const tables1 = [t1, t3, t5, t7, t8, t9];
118.        tables1.forEach((tab) => {
119.           tab.getCell(0, 1).getChild(0).asParagraph()
120.              .setAttributes(s0);
121.        });
```

L117: Add the tables in an array.

L118-121: Iterate through the tables and apply the style to the second cell in each table.

Now, let's add the style, *s1*, to some of the other tables.

```
123.        const tables2 = [t2, t4, t6];
124.        tables2.forEach((tab) => {
125.           tab.getCell(0, 1).getChild(0).asParagraph()
126.              .setAttributes(s1);
127.        });
```

L123: Add the tables to an array.

L124-127: Iterate through the tables and apply the style to the second cell in each table.

```
129.        //Add additional page
130.        body.appendPageBreak();
131.
132.        //Add quotes to rows without link
133.        shCerts.getRange(sRow + 1, linkCol + 1).setValue('----- " -----');
134.      }
135.      //save edits
136.      openCert.saveAndClose();
137.    }
```

L130: As this is going to be a multiple-page document, at the end we need to add a page break, to get the document ready for another page on a fresh page.

L133: We're going to add a document link to the first student in the list of students on the Google sheet, but for the rest we're going to add '----- " -----' to show it's part of that document. To do so, we get the current array index and add 1 to get the row number, then get the column number by getting the array index and also adding 1.

L134: We close the for loop from line 11.

L136-137: Finally, we save and close the document, and close the function.

Script 4
Add the link to the document on the sheet and move the document

```
1. function updateSheet(newCertId, certFolder, startRowNum,
2.    endRowNum, shCerts, ss) {
3.    //Move Doc
4.    const newDoc = DriveApp.getFileById(newCertId);
5.    newDoc.moveTo(certFolder);
```

L1-2: Open the function and pass the new document ID, the folder, the start and end row numbers, the certificates sheet and the spreadsheet.

L4-5: Get the file by its ID, then move it to the certificates folder.

```
7. //Add cert URL to Sheet
8. const noOfCerts = (endRowNum - startRowNum) + 1;
9. const cell = shCerts.getRange(startRowNum, 8);
10.     cell.setFormula('=HYPERLINK("https://docs.google.com/document/d/'
11.     + newCertId +
12.     '/edit";"' + noOfCerts + ' Certificates")');
13.     ss.toast("Certificates made.", "Finished", 3);
14.     }
```

L8: I want to add how many certificates are in the document. We can do that by getting the difference between the end and start row numbers and adding 1.

L9: I want to add the link in the start row, so we get that cell.

L10-12: Add the hyperlink in the cell, by setting the HYPERLINK formula, adding the file ID, then adding "/edit". Then I want to show how many certificates there are using the *noOfCerts* variable.

L13: Finally, we tell the user the program has finished and the certificates have been made.

Script 5
This script adds a menu to run the main script from.

```
1. function onOpen() {
2. const ui = SpreadsheetApp.getUi();
3. ui.createMenu('CERTIFICATES')
4. .addItem('Make Certificates', 'makeCerts')
5. .addToUi();
6. }
```

This is the same chunk of code we've seen in previous examples. Tip: I store chunks of code like these in a folder on my Drive, so I can copy and paste them into scripts, so I don't have to type it all out again.

OK let's run an example.

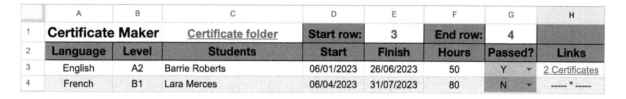

	A	B	C	D	E	F	G	H
1	**Certificate Maker**		Certificate folder	Start row:	3	End row:	4	
2	Language	Level	Students	Start	Finish	Hours	Passed?	Links
3	English	A2	Barrie Roberts	06/01/2023	26/06/2023	50	Y	2 Certificates
4	French	B1	Lara Merces	06/04/2023	31/07/2023	80	N	----- " -----

We enter the details and the row numbers we want to make.

Then we run the script from the CERTIFICATES menu.

This makes the Google Doc.

On the sheet we can open it by hovering over the link and then clicking on it.

> CONFIRMS THE ATTENDANCE OF
>
> **Barrie Roberts**
>
> COMPLETING THE COURSE
>
> **English**
>
> PASSING THE LEVEL
>
> **A2**
>
> CONSISTING OF A TOTAL OF **50.0** HOURS
>
> FROM **06/01/2023** TO **26/06/2023**
>
> DIRECTOR OF STUDIES   TEACHER

As we can see, on the first page it's created a certificate for the student that has passed.

> CONFIRMS THE ATTENDANCE OF
>
> **Lara Merces**
>
> COMPLETING THE COURSE
>
> **French**
>
> LEVEL
>
> **B1**
>
> CONSISTING OF A TOTAL OF **80.0** HOURS
>
> FROM **06/04/2023** TO **31/07/2023**
>
> DIRECTOR OF STUDIES   TEACHER

On the second page, it's created one for a student that has only completed the course. We can then print these out onto our nice-looking certificate paper. You could make a digital version just by adding the certificate background to the Google Doc template. You could then email them from the Sheet similar to the reports we sent out in the last chapter.

9: Email specific conference information
Google Forms version

In this chapter, we're going to create a form which will be embedded on a Google Site, where the user can request specific information about various conference talks. They fill in the form and they will receive the information for the talks they have selected.

Overview

1) On a Google Site, the user fills in a Google Form requesting specific information on a range of talks to be sent to them.
2) When the form is submitted, the script will get the relevant information from the Sheet and then email them that specific information as a PDF attachment.

Key learning points

1) How to get the latest form submission.
2) How to filter sheet content by the form responses.
3) How to insert an inline image into a Google Doc.
4) How to append a list.
5) How to style that list: indent, line spacing, bullet type (glyph type)

First, let's look at the form, the sheet, the email and the final PDF that will be produced.

Form

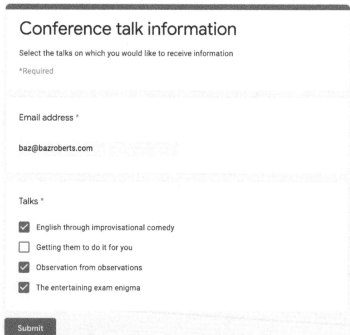

The user enters their email address and then selects the talks they want. This is embedded on a Google Site.

Sheet

The form submissions will appear here, although we won't be using the sheet to create the document, as it will run directly from the form. However, this will give us a record of which talks have been requested and how many people have requested information.

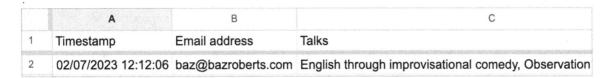

	A	B	C
1	Timestamp	Email address	Talks
2	02/07/2023 12:12:06	baz@bazroberts.com	English through improvisational comedy, Observation

On a separate sheet, we have the talk information. Each row is a talk. It contains the talk title, the speaker, the photo of the speaker, the time, the room.

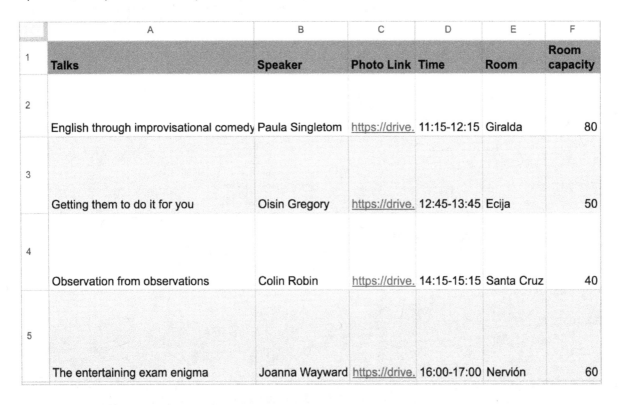

	A	B	C	D	E	F
1	Talks	Speaker	Photo Link	Time	Room	Room capacity
2	English through improvisational comedy	Paula Singletom	https://drive.	11:15-12:15	Giralda	80
3	Getting them to do it for you	Oisin Gregory	https://drive.	12:45-13:45	Ecija	50
4	Observation from observations	Colin Robin	https://drive.	14:15-15:15	Santa Cruz	40
5	The entertaining exam enigma	Joanna Wayward	https://drive.	16:00-17:00	Nervión	60

Plus, the room capacity, the talk type, the target audience, and the talk blurb.

Talk Type	Target Audience	Talk Blurb
Workshop	All teachers	This talk will focus on several improvisation comedy games by briefly describing them in a slide-show and by demonstrating how they are played. The games are taught in order to help students to talk in a much more spontaneous, fun and natural way. There will be a lot of audience participation which should make the talk more interesting and memorable.
Workshop	Teachers with < 2 years' of experience	Ever find yourself feeling you spend too much time preparing content that perhaps your students could make for you? From getting students to make their own quizzes, encouraging them to make their own activities, using English outside the class, to even getting the parents involved with revision - there is something for everyone from students aged 12 and up.
Talk	Teachers with < 4 years' of experience	Observations play a vital role during the year for the development of teachers, but what information have we collected and how can we use this to improve the delivery of lessons from those observed? This session will provide a look at the areas, which have been regularly identified during observations, with a focus on how we can provide support and training through practical ideas and solutions.
Workshop	Teachers with > 5 years' of experience	Teaching exam preparation classes is a requirement for many teachers nowadays, but dull, dry and depressing don't have to describe your classes. This workshop will take a look at how we can liven up our exam preparation courses with a variety of ideas, activities and adaptation of authentic materials. We'll deal briefly with both Cambridge and Trinity exams while also considering tasks that can be used with a broader spectrum of classes and groups.

Email and document

When the user has submitted the form, they will receive this email.

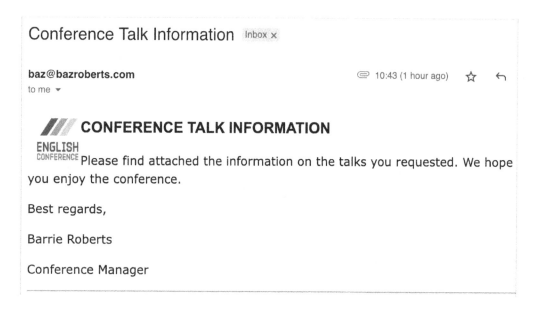

Attached is a PDF with the information on the talks they have selected.

ENGLISH
CONFERENCE

- Talk: English through improvisational comedy

- Speaker: Paula Singletom

- Time: 11:15-12:15

- Room: Giralda - Capacity: 80 people

- Type: Workshop

- Target audience: All teachers

This talk will focus on several improvisation comedy games by briefly describing them in a slide-show and by demonstrating how they are played. The games are taught in order to help students to talk in a much more spontaneous, fun and natural way. There will be a lot of audience participation which should make the talk more interesting and memorable.

The code

There are 4 script files and 1 HTML file in this project.

1-getFormSubmission – This gets the talks the user has chosen and their email address.

2-getTalkInfo – This gets the information related to the talks they have chosen.

3-addTalksToDoc – This adds the talk information to a newly-created document.

4-sendTalkInfo – This emails the document as a PDF to the user.

5-email.html – This is the email template.

These are bound to the form, i.e. open the script editor in the form and add the code there.

Script 1
Getting the form submission details

```
1. //Get talks from form submission
2. function getFormSubmission(e) {
3.   const form = FormApp.getActiveForm();
```

```
4.
5.    //Get list of talks selected
6.    const lastRespNo = form.getResponses().length - 1;
7.    const latestResp = form.getResponses()[lastRespNo];
8.    const talksSelected = latestResp.getItemResponses()[0]
9.                                    .getResponse();
```

L2: Open the function and pass the form event 'e' as a parameter.

L3: Get the active form.

L6: We want the latest response so we get the length of all of the form responses minus one to get the last array position.

L7: Then get the responses at that position, i.e. the last one.

L8: Then we need to get the item in that response, i.e. the question the user filled out. There is only one question, so this will be at index 0 in our *latestResp* array. Note, the email field isn't included in this.

L9: We then get the response to that question, which will be an array of talks they have chosen.

```
11.    //Get talk info and add to Google Doc
12.    const talkInfoSelected = getTalkInfo(talksSelected);
13.    const doc = addTalksToDoc(talkInfoSelected);
```

L12: We then call the **getTalkInfo()** function and pass the talks selected to it. The returned value will be stored in *talkInfoSelected*. See script 2 for more details.

L14: We then call the **addTalksToDoc()** function and pass the talk info selected to it. The returned value is the document we're going to send. See script 3 for more details.

```
15.    //Send email
16.    const userEmail = e.response.getRespondentEmail();
17.    sendTalkInfo(userEmail, doc);
```

L16: We get the user's email from the **e** event.

L17: We call the **sendTalkInfo()** function and pass the user's email and the document to it.

```
19.    //Delete Doc from Drive
20.    const document = DriveApp.getFileById(doc.getId());
21.    document.setTrashed(true);
22.    }
```

L20: We don't need the document that was created on our Drive, so we're going to move it to the trash. Get the file by its ID.

L21-22: Then **setTrashed()** is true to move it to the trash. Then close the function.

Script 2
Get talk details from sheet

```
1. //Get info on talks selected
2. function getTalkInfo(talksSelected) {
3.    const ss = SpreadsheetApp.openById('FILE ID');
4.    const shTalkInfo = ss.getSheetByName('TALKINFO');
5.    const talkInfo = shTalkInfo.getDataRange().getValues();
6.    talkInfo.shift();
```

L2-4: Open the function, get the spreadsheet holding the talk info, and the sheet called TALKINFO.

L5-6: We then get the data on that sheet and remove the header row.

Now, we need to get the talk info for just the talks that the user selected.

```
8. const talkInfoSelected = talkInfo.map((talk) => {
9.    return talk;
10.       })
11.        .filter((talk) => {
12.          return talksSelected.includes(talk[0]) === true;
13.       });
14.    return talkInfoSelected;
15.    }
```

L8-10: We then iterate through the talk info with **map()** and extract the talk titles.

L11-13: We then filter those talks which are in the *talksSelected* array. We do that by getting the talk title in the first position and using the includes method to see if it exists somewhere in the *talksSelected* array. If it does, it keeps it if not it's filtered out.

L14: This is then returned back to script 1 and line 12.

Script 3
Add talks info to Google Doc

```
1. //Create Doc and add talk info to it
2. function addTalksToDoc(talkInfoSelected) {
```

```
3.
4.      //Create doc and add header
5.      const doc = DocumentApp.create('Conference Talk Information');
6.      const body = doc.getBody();
7.      doc.addHeader();
8.      const header = doc.getHeader();
9.      const confLogo = DriveApp.getFileById('FILE ID').getBlob();
10.         const hparas = header.getParagraphs();
11.         hparas[0].insertInlineImage(0, confLogo);
```

L2: Open the function and pass the talk info selected.
L5-6: Create a new Google Doc. Then get its body.

We're going to add the conference logo in the header.

L7-8: We first need to add the header. Then get that header.

L9: Then get the logo image by its ID and then get its blob.

L10: We then get the paragraphs in the header.

L11: Then get the first paragraph (there's only one) and insert the image. In the brackets we set the child index as 0 and pass the image blob.

Next, let's set up the styling for the text.

```
13.         const style1 = {};
14.         style1[DocumentApp.Attribute.FONT_FAMILY] = 'Calibri';
15.         style1[DocumentApp.Attribute.FONT_SIZE] = 16;
16.         style1[DocumentApp.Attribute.BOLD] = true;
17.
18.         const style2 = {};
19.         style2[DocumentApp.Attribute.HORIZONTAL_ALIGNMENT]
20.             = DocumentApp.HorizontalAlignment.JUSTIFY;
```

L13: We set up the *style1* object.

L14-16: Then set the font, font-size, and bolding.

L18-20: Set up the *style2* object and add the justify alignment.

Next, we need to iterate through the talks and add the data about them to the document.

```
22.      //Loop thru talks
23.      talkInfoSelected.forEach((talkSel) => {
```

```
24.        [talk, speaker, image, time, room,
25.          capacity, type, audience, blurb] = talkSel;
```

L23: Iterate through the talk info selected.

L24-25: Destructure the *talkSel* array and assign the variables.

Now, let's get the speaker image.

```
28.        //Add speaker image
29.        const fileID = image.match(/[\w\_\-]{25,}/).toString();
30.        const blob = DriveApp.getFileById(fileID).getBlob();
31.        body.appendImage(blob);
```

L29: We extract the file ID from the file URL for the speaker image using a regular expression.

L30: We then get that file as a blob.

L31: Then append it to the body.

We get the talk information which will be added to the body as a bulleted list.

```
33.        const allListInfo = ["Talk: " + talk, "Speaker: " + speaker,
34.        "Time: " + time,
35.        "Room: " + room + " - Capacity: " + capacity + " people",
36.        "Type: " + type, "Target audience: " + audience];
37.
38.        allListInfo.forEach((info) => {
39.          body.appendListItem(info)
40.            .setIndentStart(0)
41.            .setLineSpacing(2)
42.            .setGlyphType(DocumentApp.GlyphType.SQUARE_BULLET)
43.            .setAttributes(style1);
44.        });
```

L33-36: We set up an array of all the pieces of information.

L38: We then iterate through that array to create the list.

L39: Append each item using **appendListItem()**.

L40: We can set the indent start. If it's 0, it's not necessary, but I've left it in here so you can see how it would work.

L41: I want double line spacing, so we pass 2 to **setLineSpacing()**.

L42: I want to add square bullets. To do so, we set the glyph type.

L43: Finally, we apply the styling to the text.

I want the blurb to be aligned using justify and in between horizontal lines.

```
46.          body.appendHorizontalRule();
47.          body.appendParagraph(blurb).setAttributes(style2);
48.          body.appendHorizontalRule();
49.          body.appendPageBreak();
50.        });
```

L46: We add a horizontal rule.

L47: We then add the blurb as a paragraph and set the styling.

L48: We add another horizontal rule.

L49: We add a page break, ready for the next talk information.

L50: We close the **forEach()** method on the *talkInfoSelected* array.

```
52.        doc.saveAndClose();
53.        return doc;
54.      }
```

L52-54: We then save and close the document and return it back to script 1 and line 13.

Script 4
Email talk info as a PDF attachment

```
1.  //Email talk info to user
2.  function sendTalkInfo(userEmail, doc) {
3.    const emailBody = HtmlService.createHtmlOutputFromFile('email')
4.                              .getContent();
```

L2: We open the function and pass the user's email and the document.

L3-4: We use the **HtmlService** to create the email body from the file called 'email'. Make sure you get its content.

```
6.  //Get G Doc and make a PDF then attach
7.  const pdf = doc.getAs('application/pdf').getBytes();
8.  const attach = {
```

```
9.        fileName: 'Conference Talk Information.pdf',
10.       content: pdf,
11.       mimeType: 'application/pdf'
12.       };
```

L7: Get the document as a PDF.

L8-12: Create the attachment by setting the **filename**, the **content**, and the **mimeType** and storing that as an object in *attach*.

```
14.       const image = DriveApp.getFileById("FILE ID").getBlob();
15.       MailApp.sendEmail(userEmail, "Conference Talk Information", '',
16.       {
17.         htmlBody: emailBody,
18.         replyTo: 'baz@bazroberts.com',
19.         inlineImages: { logo: image },
20.         attachments: [attach]
21.       });
22.       }
```

L14: Get the conference image as a blob.

L15: We use **MailApp** to send the email and pass the user's email and the email title, and leave the email body blank, as we're going to use the HTML to create it.

L16-22: We set up the HTML body and the properties.

HTML file
Email template

```
1. <!DOCTYPE html>
2. <html>
3. <head>
4.    <base target="_top">
```

L1-3: State it's a HTML document and open the html and head tags.

L4: Set the default action of clicking on a link.

```
6.    <style>
7.      p {
8.        font-family: verdana;
9.        font-size: 1.2em;
10.       }
11.
```

```
12.         #image {
13.            float: left;
14.            width: 60px;
15.            height: 60px;
16.            padding-left: 10px;
17.          }
18.        </style>
19.      </head>
```

L5: Open the style tag.

L6-10: Set up the styling for the paragraphs in the email.

L12-19: We set up the styling for the conference talk logo in the email. Then close the style and head tags.

```
21.      <body>
22.        <div>
23.          <img id="image" src=cid:logo>
24.          <h2>CONFERENCE TALK INFORMATION</h2>
25.          <p>Please find attached the information on the talks you
     requested.
26.             We hope you enjoy the conference.</p>
27.          <p>Best regards,</p>
28.          <p>Barrie Roberts</p>
29.          <p>Conference Manager</p>
30.          <hr>
31.        </div>
32.      </body>
33.
34.      </html>
```

L21-22: Open the body tag and create a div.

L23: Add the conference logo image using the logo variable and style it with the image ID.

L24-29: Add the title and the email text.

L30: Add a horizontal rule.

L31-34: Close the div, body and html tags.

Trigger

Before running it, we need to set up the **on Form Submit** trigger.

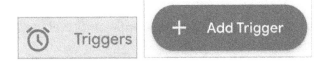

Click on the clock symbol then click "Add trigger".

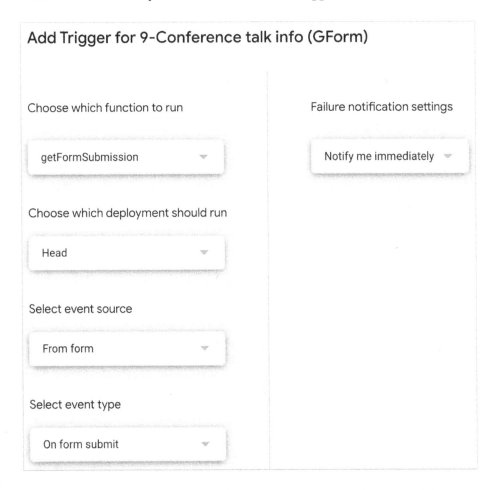

Add Trigger for 9-Conference talk info (GForm)

Choose which function to run

> getFormSubmission ▼

Choose which deployment should run

> Head ▼

Select event source

> From form ▼

Select event type

> On form submit ▼

Failure notification settings

> Notify me immediately ▼

Select the "On form submit" event type. I usually want to be notified immediately of any problems. Then click Save.

Triggers

+ Add a filter

Owned by	Last run	Deployment	Event	Function
Me	-	Head	From form - On form submit	getFormSubmission

The trigger will then be set up. Close the window.

Add Google Form to a Google Site

We're going to add our Google Form in a Google Site, so users can go to the conference web page and fill out the form.

Open the Google Site, go to the page you want, and click on "Insert".

Then near the bottom of the list, click on Forms.

This will give you a selection of forms to insert and as it's sorted by date and time, the one you want should be at the top.

Then click Insert.

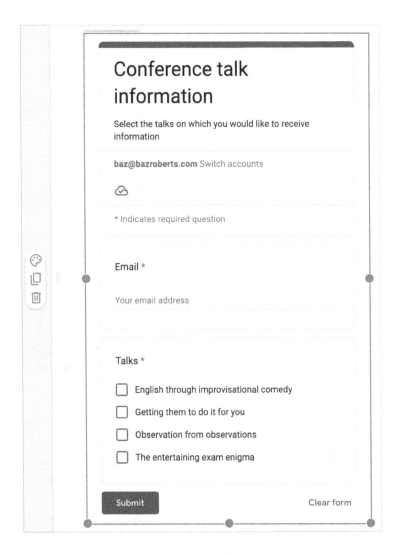

This will embed the Google Form into the web page. Publish the Google Site, so that people can see the form.

For more info on working with Google Sites, check out my Step-by-step Guide to Google Sites. :)

Ok, let's try it out. We fill in the form with our email address and tick the conference talk we're interested in.

We then receive an email with the information on the talks attached as a PDF.

baz@bazroberts.com   10:43 (1 hour ago) ☆ ↩

to me ▾

 CONFERENCE TALK INFORMATION

ENGLISH
CONFERENCE Please find attached the information on the talks you requested. We hope you enjoy the conference.

Best regards,

Barrie Roberts

Conference Manager

Opening the PDF, we see we have the information on the talks we selected.

- **Talk: Observation from observations**

- **Speaker: Colin Robin**

- **Time: 14:15-15:15**

- **Room: Santa Cruz - Capacity: 40 people**

- **Type: Talk**

- **Target audience: Teachers with < 4 years' of experience**

Observations play a vital role during the year for the development of teachers, but what information have we collected and how can we use this to improve the delivery of lessons from those observed? This session will provide a look at the areas, which have been regularly identified during observations, with a focus on how we can provide support and training through practical ideas and solutions.

- **Talk: The entertaining exam enigma**

- **Speaker: Joanna Wayward**

- **Time: 16:00-17:00**

- **Room: Nervión - Capacity: 60 people**

- **Type: Workshop**

- **Target audience: Teachers with > 5 years' of experience**

Teaching exam preparation classes is a requirement for many teachers nowadays, but dull, dry and depressing don't have to describe your classes. This workshop will take a look at how we can liven up our exam preparation courses with a variety of ideas, activities and adaptation of authentic materials. We'll deal briefly with both Cambridge and Trinity exams while also considering tasks that can be used with a broader spectrum of classes and groups.

10: Sending conference info via a web app
HTML form version

In this chapter, we're going to send the same talk information as we saw in the previous chapter, except this time we're going to create our own HTML form and get the submission.

The main benefit of this is that we can style the form exactly how we want it and it can look more professional rather than relying on a Google one.

Plus, the main reason we're going to do this here is to learn how to create a web app, in this case a form, and how we get data from that app to use elsewhere. Learning this will open a whole new world to you and enable you to do far more with Apps Script.

Overview

1) We get the talk info from the Google Sheet.
2) We then build our form and use the talk info to create the options in the form.
3) The form template is stored as a HTML file. We are using a library from the **materializecss.com** website to simplify the styling part.
4) We use an event listener to listen for the Send button being clicked.
5) We get the email address and the talk fields and whether they have been checked or not.
6) We then send that data to then get the relevant talk info.
7) We add that talk info to a newly-created document, as we saw in chapter 9.
8) We then send an email to the user, with the talk info attached.
9) Finally, we reset the form.

Key learning points

1) How to use **doGet()** to create web apps.
2) How to build a form dynamically.
3) How to use the materialize library.
4) How to use event listeners on forms.
5) How to get and store multiple form information.
6) How to use **google.script.run** to send data back into your script.

First, let's look at the form we'll be creating. The email and the final talk info PDF is the same as in the previous chapter.

Form

As you can see, this form is quite different from a standard Google Form.

The code

Create a new script file in your Drive. In this project we have 4 script files and 3 HTML files:

1createForm.gs: This gets the talk information and creates the form. – **doGet(), include()**

2form.html: This contains the form template.

3getFormSub.html: This gets the data from the form and runs the **getTalkInfo()** function. It also resets the form once the data has been sent and processed.

4getTalkInfo.gs: This gets the talk info from the Google Sheet, similar to what we saw in chapter 9. – **getTalkInfo()**

5addTalksToDoc.gs: This creates the document with the talk info. This is the same as what we saw in chapter 9. – **addTalksToDoc()**

6sendTalkInfo.gs: This sends the email with the talk info PDF as an attachment. This is the same as chapter 9. – **sendTalkInfo()**

7email.html: This is the HTML template for the email. Again, the same as chapter 9.

Script 1
1createForm.gs - Get the talk data and create the form

```
1.  function doGet() {
2.    //Get talks
3.    const ssConf = SpreadsheetApp.openById('FILE ID');
4.    const shTalkInfo = ssConf.getSheetByName('TALKINFO');
5.    const allTalkInfo = shTalkInfo.getDataRange().getValues();
6.    allTalkInfo.shift();
```

L1: To run a web app we need to use the function name **doGet()**.

L3-4: We get the spreadsheet holding the talk info and get the sheet called TALKINFO.

L5-6: We then get the sheet data and remove the header row.

```
8.    //Build form
9.    const formTmp = HtmlService.createTemplateFromFile('2form');
```

L9: We create the form first by getting the HTML template stored in the file '2form'. Note, we're using the **createTemplateFromFile()** method here.

We need to populate our form with the talk choices in our sheet. Before we look at the details, let's just look at a simplified hard-coded version, so you can see what I'm aiming to achieve.

```
<p>
  <label>
  <input type"checkbox" class="indeterminate-checkbox"/>
  <span>The entertaining exam enigma</span>
  </label>
</p>
```

Here, we use the paragraph tags as each option will be on a new line.
We then set the input type as a checkbox and as we're using Materialize we name the class as "indeterminate-checkbox" to achieve the effect we want.
We then use a span tag to add the text we want in-line with the checkbox.

```
10.      formTmp.talks = allTalkInfo.map((talkInfo, n) => {
11.        return '<p><label><input id="CB'
12.        + n
13.        + '" type="checkbox" class="indeterminate-checkbox"/><span>'
14.        + talkInfo[0] +'</span></label></p>'
15.      }).join('');
16.
```

```
17.        return formTmp.evaluate();
18.      }
```

L10: So, to add all the talk titles, we loop through the *allTalkInfo* array. We use **map()** to do this as we'll be returning the result into the object property *formTmp.talks*.

Each loop will create a chunk of HTML code like this:

```
<p><label><input id="CB0" type="checkbox" class="indeterminate-
checkbox"/><span>English through improvisational comedy</span></label>
</p>

<p><label><input id="CB1" type="checkbox" class="indeterminate-
checkbox"/><span>Getting them to do it for you</span></label></p>

<p><label><input id="CB2" type="checkbox" class="indeterminate-
checkbox"/><span>Observation from observations</span></label></p>

<p><label><input id="CB3" type="checkbox" class="indeterminate-
checkbox"/><span>The entertaining exam enigma</span></label></p>
```

L11: We put each talk title in a paragraph.
The label tag allows the user to click on the text and the checkbox still to be selected.
The checkbox is a type of input and we give an ID of "CB".
Also, we will have several checkboxes, we will need to individually identify them to see whether they have been checked or not. So, we can use the map index n to number the ID, i.e. CB0, CB1, etc.

L12: We then state the input type is a checkbox and give it a class so that Materialize knows what style to give it. We then open the <Span> tag so that the title text is inline with the checkbox.

L13: We add the talk title text.

L14: We close the <span>, <label> and <p> tag, and close the map loop. This all produces a piece of HTML, which we then join together to create one long piece of HTML.

This is all stored in *formTmp.talks*. As we will see below, we will be able to access the *talks* property in the form HTML and be able to add the checklists to the form, just by calling the *talks* property.

L16: We then need to evaluate the template.

```
22.      function include(filename) {
23.        return HtmlService.createHtmlOutputFromFile(filename)
24.                      .getContent();
25.      }
```

L22: In the HTML file we will call some script stored in another HTML file. To do that, we need to include a little function called **include()** and pass the filename as a parameter.

L23-24: We use the **createHtmlOutputFromFile()** method to do this and get its content.

HTML 1
2form.html - The form HTML template

```
1. <!DOCTYPE html>
2. <html>
3.   <head>
4.     <base target="_top">
5.     <link href="https://fonts.googleapis.com/icon?family=Material+Icons"
   rel="stylesheet">
6.     <meta name="viewport" content="width=device-width, initial-scale=1.0"/>
7.     <link rel="stylesheet"
8. href="https://cdnjs.cloudflare.com/ajax/libs/materialize/1.0.0/css/materiali
   ze.min.css">
9.   </head>
```

L1-4: Set the document type, open the html and head tags.

Then we get the libraries we're going to use. The Google icons one and the materialize one.

L5: This line taken from: https://google.github.io/material-design-icons/
This will provide the send button icon.

L6: This line will make the page responsive to the screen size, so it will match the browser window pixel width to the pixel width of the screen. I got this from here: https://css-tricks.com/snippets/html/responsive-meta-tag/

L7-8: This is the CSS library for materialize, taken from their website here: https://materializecss.com/getting-started.html

L9: We close the head tag.

```
11.       <body>
12.         <div class="container">
13.           <div class="row">
14.             <h3 class="card-panel blue darken-4 white-text">CONFERENCE
   TALKS</h3>
15.           </div>
```

L11: We open the body tag.

L12: We create a div to contain the title and form.

L13: We create a div for the row we are creating. Materialize needs the div to have the class name "row".

L14: Here, we add the title. In the <h3> tag we add a class to then dictate what we want. Here I want a solid rectangle, which is called a card panel, fill it with a dark blue colour, and use white text.

L15: We close that row div.

```
17.        <form>
18.        <div class="row" class="input-field col s12">
19.          <input type="email" id="emailAdd">
20.          <label>Email address</label>
21.        </div>
```

L17: Here, we open our form.

First, we add the email address field.

L18: We add another div and make it a row. We also set it as an input field and set the column size as 12, which means it will fill the whole div.

L19: We add the input, its type, and give it the ID "emailAdd".

L20: Then add a label underneath.

L21: Close the div.

Here, we add the checkboxes and talk titles.

```
23.        <div id="talksCBs" class="row" class="input-field col s12"
    class="checkbox">
24.          <?!= talks; ?>
25.        </div>
26.        </form>
```

L23: We open another div and give it the ID "talksCBs". We set it as another row, set it as an input field and we want it to stretch across the div if necessary and we state it's a checkbox.

L24: This is where we add the HTML we created in script 1 and had stored in *formTmp.talks*. We use scriptlet tags (<?!= ?>) to allow us to add the property from the first script. Note, as we're going to use the HTML to show content on the page, we use it with the exclamation mark and equals sign.

L25-26: We close this div and the form.

```
28.        <div class="row">
29.          <button id="btn" class="btn-small blue darken-4 col s2">
30.          <i class="material-icons left">send</i>SEND</button>
31.        </div>
32.      </div> <!--CLOSE CONTAINER-->
```

The final part is to add a submit/send button.

L28: Add a new row.

L29: We add a button, give it the ID "btn". Then I want a small dark blue button that we only take up 2 out of 12 columns.

L30: Use the <i> tag to add an icon from the Google icon library. Here, I want a send symbol. We then close the button tag.

L31-32: We then close this div and the overall containing div.

```
34.        <script
     src="https://cdnjs.cloudflare.com/ajax/libs/materialize/1.0.0/js/materialize
     .min.js"></script>
```

L34: Here we load the JavaScript library from materialize. Best practice is to load all the visible parts first then the JavaScript at the end.

```
36.        <?!= include('3getFormSub'); ?>
37.      </body>
38.      </html>
```

L36: We want to include the JavaScript in another HTML file. To do so, we use the *include* function we set up in script 1 and call the name of the script file. As this is JavaScript, we need to include this in the scriptlet tags.

L37-38: We then close the body and html tags.

HTML 2
3getFormSub.html - Interacting with the form

Even though this is a HTML file, it's in fact all JavaScript and we place all of it within <script> tags.

```
1.  <script>
2.    //Initiate - Materialize
3.    document.addEventListener('DOMContentLoaded', function() {
4.      const elems =
    document.querySelectorAll('input[type="checkbox"].checkbox');
5.      const instances = M.FormSelect.init(elems);
6.  });
```

L1: We open the <script> tag.

L3-6: This is a script taken from the **materializecss** website here: https://materializecss.com/select.html to initiate the library. Note, the **querySelectorAll()** part has to be updated as per the code above for checkboxes. Also, I've removed the options part as it's unnecessary.

Next, we set up an event listener to 'hear' if the send button is clicked.

```
8.    //Listen for send button click
9.    document.getElementById("btn")
10.         .addEventListener("click", sendInfoFromForm);
```

L9: We get the element by its ID.

L10: Then add the click event listener. If it's clicked, it will call the **sendInfoFromForm()** function.

Now, we need to get the data from the form.

```
12. function sendInfoFromForm(){
13.    //Store multiple form info
14.    const cbDiv = document.getElementById("talksCBs");
15.    const numOfCBs = cbDiv.getElementsByTagName("P").length;
```

L12: Open the function.

L14: Get the checkboxes div by its ID.

L15: Then get the number of paragraphs in that div by getting the length of the array of the <p> elements.

We now need to get the email address and to check if the checkboxes are checked or not and then store those true or false values in an array.

```
17.    //Get email address and talk status (ticked or not)
18.    const userEmail = document.getElementById("emailAdd").value;
19.    let tInfo = [];
```

```
20.   for(let i=0;i<numOfCBs;i++){
21.      tInfo.push(document.getElementById("CB"+i).checked);
22.   }
```

L18: We first get the email address by getting the value of the email address element.

L19: We create an empty array to store the true and false values from the checkboxes.

L20: We then create a loop to get whether each checkbox has been checked or not.

L21: We check if they have been selected and push either the true or false into the array.

We now need to run some more scripts on the Apps Script side (server side).

```
24.        //Send to Apps Script side
25.        google.script.run.getTalkInfo(tInfo, userEmail);
```

L25: To do this we use **google.script.run** followed by the function name we want to run, in this case the **getTalkInfo()** function. We pass the *tInfo* array and the user's email address.

That will go off and get the talk info and create the document, etc similar to what we saw in chapter 9. We'll go through that code later.

To finish this part, once the send button is clicked and the data is sent, we also want to reset our form, so the user knows something has happened. We could also add a confirmation message here.

```
27.        //Reset form
28.        document.getElementById("emailAdd").value = "";
29.        for(let j=0;j<numOfCBs;j++){
30.           document.getElementById("CB"+j).checked = false;
31.        }
32.        M.updateTextFields();
33.     }
34.  </script>
```

L28: We get the email address field and set it to blank.

L29: We then loop through the checkboxes and reset each one to false, i.e. unticked.

L30: With materialize we also need to use **M.updateTextFields()** to carry out the above.

L31: We close our <script> tag.

Script 2
4getTalkInfo.gs - Get the talk info

This function is called from the **google.script.run** on line 25 in *3getFormSub*. Some of this script is the same as what we saw in chapter 9. I'll explain in more detail the parts that aren't.

```
1.  //Get info on talks selected.
2.  function getTalkInfo(tInfo, userEmail) {
3.    const ss = SpreadsheetApp.openById('FILE ID');
4.    const shTalkInfo = ss.getSheetByName('TALKINFO');
5.    const talkInfo = shTalkInfo.getDataRange().getValues();
6.    talkInfo.shift();
```

L2-6: We pass the talk info true or false array and the email address to the function. We then get the talk info from the sheet and get the data.

```
8.        //Get all talk titles
9.        const talkTitles = talkInfo.map((talk) => {
10.         return talk[0];
11.       });
```

L9-11: Get the talk titles from the *talkInfo* array.

```
13.        //If true get talk title
14.        let listOfTalks = [];
15.        tInfo.forEach((ti, n) => {
16.          if (ti === true) {
17.            listOfTalks.push(talkTitles[n]);
18.          }
19.        });
```

L14: Set up a blank array to store the talk titles the user wants.

L15: We then loop through the checkbox T/F options.

L16-18: If it is true, then we push the relevant talk title into the *listOfTalks* array.

```
21.        //Get talk info for talks selected
22.        const talkInfoSelected = talkInfo.map((talk) => {
23.          return talk;
24.        })
25.          .filter((talk) => {
26.            return listOfTalks.includes(talk[0]) === true;
27.          });
```

L22-27: We then get the talk info related to those talk titles by mapping through the list of talks and storing the ones which appear in the array *listOfTalks*.

```
29.        //Add talks to doc and send talks to user
30.        const doc = addTalksToDoc(talkInfoSelected);
31.        sendTalkInfo(userEmail, doc);
```

L30: Then call the **addTalksToDoc()** function passing the *talkInfoSelected* array. It will return the document. See script 3 below.

L31: Call the **sendTalkInfo()** function and pass the user's email address and the document. See script 4 below.

Script 3
5addTalksToDoc.gs - Add the talk info to the document

This is the same as the function in chapter 9. Here's the code.

```
1.  //Create Doc and add talk info to it (same as C9: 3-addTalksToDoc)
2.  function addTalksToDoc(talkInfoSelected) {
3.
4.      //Create doc and add header
5.      const doc = DocumentApp.create('Conference Talk Information');
6.      const body = doc.getBody();
7.      doc.addHeader();
8.      const header = doc.getHeader();
9.      const confLogo = DriveApp.getFileById('FILE ID').getBlob();
10.        const hparas = header.getParagraphs();
11.        hparas[0].insertInlineImage(0, confLogo);
12.
13.        const style1 = {};
14.        style1[DocumentApp.Attribute.FONT_FAMILY] = 'Calibri';
15.        style1[DocumentApp.Attribute.FONT_SIZE] = 16;
16.        style1[DocumentApp.Attribute.BOLD] = true;
17.
18.        const style2 = {};
19.        style2[DocumentApp.Attribute.HORIZONTAL_ALIGNMENT]
20.        = DocumentApp.HorizontalAlignment.JUSTIFY;
21.
22.        //Loop thru talks
23.        talkInfoSelected.forEach((talkSel) => {
24.
25.          [talk, speaker, image, time, room,
26.          capacity, type, audience, blurb] = talkSel;
```

```
27.
28.        //Add speaker image
29.        const fileID = image.match(/[\w\_\-]{25,}/).toString();
30.        const blob = DriveApp.getFileById(fileID).getBlob();
31.        body.appendImage(blob);
32.
33.        const allListInfo = ["Talk: " + talk, "Speaker: " + speaker,
34.        "Time: " + time,
35.        "Room: " + room + " - Capacity: " + capacity + " people",
36.        "Type: " + type, "Target audience: " + audience];
37.
38.        allListInfo.forEach((info) => {
39.          body.appendListItem(info)
40.              .setIndentStart(0)
41.              .setLineSpacing(2)
42.              .setGlyphType(DocumentApp.GlyphType.SQUARE_BULLET)
43.              .setAttributes(style1);
44.        });
45.
46.        body.appendHorizontalRule();
47.        body.appendParagraph(blurb).setAttributes(style2);
48.        body.appendHorizontalRule();
49.        body.appendPageBreak();
50.      });
51.
52.      doc.saveAndClose();
53.      return doc;
54.    }
```

Script 4

6sendTalkInfo.gs - Send the talk info in the email as a PDF attachment

This function is also the same as chapter 9. The only difference is that it calls the script file "7email" in line 3. Here's the code.

```
1. //Email talk info to user
2. function sendTalkInfo(userEmail, doc) {
3.   const emailBody = HtmlService.createHtmlOutputFromFile('7email')
4.                              .getContent();
5.
6.   //Get G Doc and make a PDF then attach
7.   const pdf = doc.getAs('application/pdf').getBytes();
8.   const attach = {
9.       fileName: 'Conference Talk Information.pdf',
```

```
10.         content: pdf,
11.         mimeType: 'application/pdf'
12.       };
13.
14.     const image = DriveApp.getFileById("FILE ID").getBlob();
15.     MailApp.sendEmail(userEmail, "Conference Talk Information", '',
16.     {
17.       htmlBody: emailBody,
18.       replyTo: 'baz@bazroberts.com',
19.       inlineImages: { logo: image },
20.       attachments: [attach]
21.     });
22.     }
```

HTML 3
7email.html - Email template

This email template is the same as chapter 9. Here's the code.

```
1.  <!DOCTYPE html>
2.  <html>
3.
4.  <head>
5.    <base target="_top">
6.    <style>
7.      p {
8.        font-family: verdana;
9.        font-size: 1.2em;
10.      }
11.
12.      #image {
13.        float: left;
14.        width: 60px;
15.        height: 60px;
16.        padding-left: 10px;
17.      }
18.    </style>
19.  </head>
20.
21.  <body>
22.    <div>
23.      <img id="image" src=cid:logo>
24.      <h2>CONFERENCE TALK INFORMATION</h2>
```

```
25.          <p>Please find attached the information on the talks you
     requested.
26.       We hope you enjoy the conference.</p>
27.          <p>Best regards,</p>
28.          <p>Barrie Roberts</p>
29.          <p>Conference Manager</p>
30.          <hr>
31.        </div>
32.      </body>
33.
34.      </html>
```

How to deploy as a web app

Now that we have all the code written we now need to deploy the project as a web app.

At the top of the script editor click on Deploy. Then select 'New deployment'.

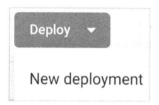

Now we need to fill in some details about the new deployment. First click on the Description box.

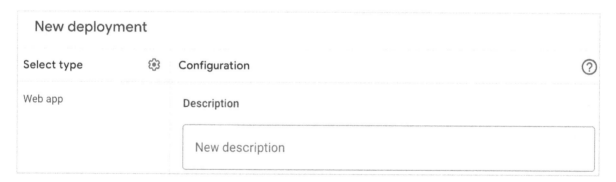

Then type in a description of your deployment. This is usual if you end up saving different versions of your project.

Underneath, leave it as executing as yourself, as we don't want users to have to log in and then authorise the script. Plus, leave the Who has access to anyone, as we want anyone to be able to use the web app.

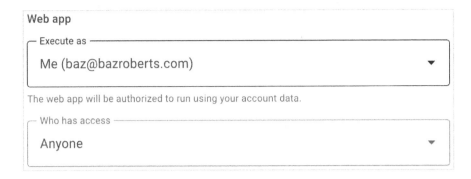

Then click the Deploy button at the bottom. It will ask you authorise access and clicking the Authorise access button will take you through the same process as authorising a script.

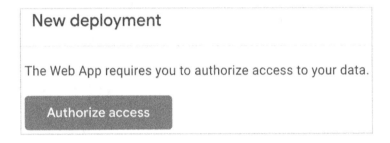

It will confirm the deployment. The URL at the bottom is the link the user will use to access the form. Click Copy.

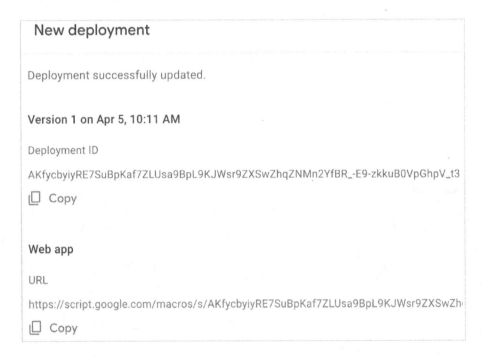

Adding the web app to a Google Site

One easy way to share your web app is to embed the URL in a Google Site.

Open the page on your Google Site and right click on the area you want to add the app. A circle with various options will appear. Click on the yellow arrows "Embed".

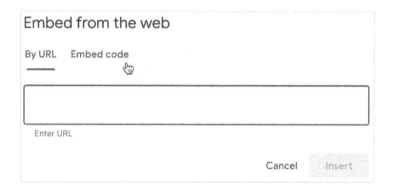

This opens a dialogue box and gives you two options to embed, choose the By URL one and paste in the URL in the box.

This will show you a preview of the web app. If it looks ok, click Insert.

CONFERENCE TALKS

Email address

☐ English through improvisational comedy

☐ Getting them to do it for you

☐ Observation from observations

☐ The entertaining exam enigma

➤ SEND

This will then add the form to the page. Then publish the web site and it's ready for people to fill out the form.

11: Update document from data on the web

In this chapter, we are going to automatically get the latest 6 Nations rugby results from Wikipedia and use the **IMPORTHTML()** function in Google Sheets. Then every Monday after the matches, the program will email the latest results and the current table.

The key idea here is how we can get data from the internet and add it to a Google Doc. Once set up it will run automatically with a trigger. It contains lots of examples of who to clean up data from an external source and to style the document.

The site we're going to access is here:
https://en.wikipedia.org/wiki/2021_Six_Nations_Championship
If you don't know anything about the rugby tournament, you can read all about it there too.

Overview

1) We create a Google Sheet and on one sheet we have multiple IMPORTHTML() functions to get the data we want from the Wikipedia site and store it on the sheet.
2) We create another sheet to grab and store the current tournament table.
3) The program is triggered every Monday to see if there have been matches and if so, to send an email with the latest results and table.
4) It gets the latest data from the sheet and formats it ready to add it to a Google Doc.
5) It adds the results data and also the flag icons for each of the countries.
6) On the second page it adds the latest table.
7) It then emails the Google Doc as a PDF.

Key learning points

1) How to trigger programs on certain dates.
2) How to replace and format web data.
3) How to add bolding to certain words in a paragraph.
4) How to use objects to store data.
5) How to insert inline images.
6) How to format data only when it is a number.
7) How to add alternative row shading in a table.
8) How to tidy up data from a web page.

First, let's look at the Wikipedia page we're getting the data from.

Wikipedia page
The data for this project is taken from this page:
https://en.wikipedia.org/wiki/2021_Six_Nations_Championship

Part of the way down the page there are the fixtures and the results are updated as the games are finished. They include the scores, the details of who scored and which type of scores they were. Note, in rugby there are 3 types of scores: a try, a conversation, and a penalty.

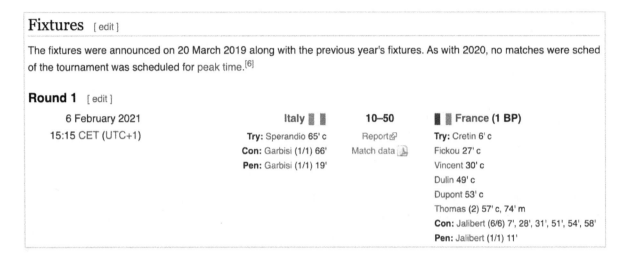

Fixtures [edit]

The fixtures were announced on 20 March 2019 along with the previous year's fixtures. As with 2020, no matches were sched of the tournament was scheduled for peak time.[6]

Round 1 [edit]

6 February 2021	Italy	10–50	France (1 BP)
15:15 CET (UTC+1)	**Try:** Sperandio 65' c **Con:** Garbisi (1/1) 66' **Pen:** Garbisi (1/1) 19'	Report Match data	**Try:** Cretin 6' c Fickou 27' c Vincent 30' c Dulin 49' c Dupont 53' c Thomas (2) 57' c, 74' m **Con:** Jalibert (6/6) 7', 28', 31', 51', 54', 58' **Pen:** Jalibert (1/1) 11'

A bit further down, you'll find the tournament table.

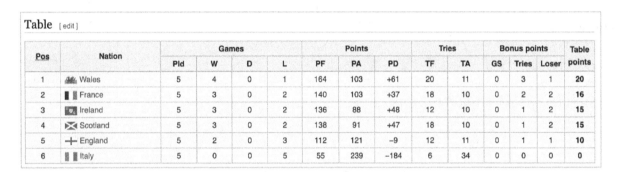

Table [edit]

Pos	Nation	Games				Points			Tries		Bonus points			Table points
		Pld	W	D	L	PF	PA	PD	TF	TA	GS	Tries	Loser	
1	Wales	5	4	0	1	164	103	+61	20	11	0	3	1	20
2	France	5	3	0	2	140	103	+37	18	10	0	2	2	16
3	Ireland	5	3	0	2	136	88	+48	12	10	0	1	2	15
4	Scotland	5	3	0	2	138	91	+47	18	10	0	1	2	15
5	England	5	2	0	3	112	121	−9	12	11	0	1	1	10
6	Italy	5	0	0	5	55	239	−184	6	34	0	0	0	0

Sheet – Results

On the Google Sheet, we have the sheet, RESULTS, to import the results data. In each white row, there is a formula which imports the data for that match.

	A	B	C
1	**Italy**	**10–50**	**France (1 BP)**
2	*Try:*Sperandio 65' c *Con:*Garbisi (1/1) 66' *Pen:*Garbisi (1/1) 19'	Report Match data	*Try:*Cretin 6' c Fickou 27' c Vincent 30' c Dulin 49' c Dupont 53' c Thomas (2) 57' c, 74' m *Con:*Jalibert (6/6) 7', 28', 31', 51', 54', 58' *Pen:*Jalibert (1/1) 11'
3	**(1 BP) England**	**6–11**	**Scotland**
4	*Pen:*Farrell (2/2) 34', 39'	Report Match data	*Try:*Van der Merwe 30' m *Pen:*Russell (2/3) 6', 49'
5	**Wales**	**21–16**	**Ireland (1 BP)**
6	*Try:*North 49' m Rees-Zammit 59' c *Con:*Halfpenny (1/2) 60' *Pen:*Halfpenny (3/3) 5', 19', 66'	Report Match data	*Try:*Beirne 37' c *Con:*Sexton (1/1) 39' *Pen:*Sexton (2/2) 29', 35' Burns (1/1) 72'

The formula uses the IMPORTHTML function. It requires a URL, the format of the data: either "list" or "table", and the index of that list or table.

```
=IMPORTHTML("https://en.wikipedia.org/wiki/2021_Six_Nations_Championship", "table", 6)
```

For the first match, we need to get the 7th table on the page (index: 6). This fills 2 rows of data. Then in row 3 we get the 14th table and so on.

Sheet – Table

On the TABLE sheet we import the tournament table.

	A	B	C	D	E	F	G	H	I	J	K	L		M	N	O
1	Pos	Nation	Games				Points			Tries		Bonus points				Table points
2			Pld		W	D	L PF	PA	PD	TF	TA	GS			Tries Loser	
3	1	Wales	5		4	0	1 164	103	+61	20	11		0	3	1	*20*
4	2	France	5		3	0	2 140	103	+37	18	10		0	2	2	*16*
5	3	Ireland	5		3	0	2 136	88	+48	12	10		0	1	2	*15*
6	4	Scotland	5		3	0	2 138	91	+47	18	10		0	1	2	*15*
7	5	England	5		2	0	3 112	121	-9	12	11		0	1	1	*10*
8	6	Italy	5		0	0	5 55	239	-184	6	34		0	0	0	*0*

We use the same function and this time get the 5th table on the page.

```
=IMPORTHTML("https://en.wikipedia.org/wiki/2021_Six_Nations_Championship", "table", 4)
```

Email

Every Monday the script will check the date to see if it should send the results and if there is a match, on the following Monday after the round of matches, it sends the following email.

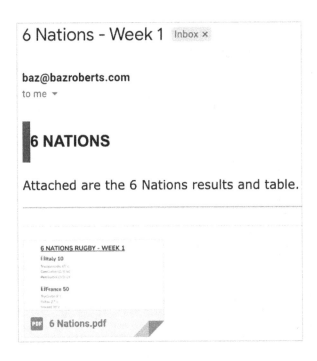

Note, this tournament runs between February and March and usually there are 5 rounds to it. So, we will receive an email for each of the weeks there are matches.

It attaches a PDF with the results and tournament table.

Results and table PDF
In the PDF we have a title and the week number. Then the first match with the country and its flag along with the score. Then underneath each country the scorers. Then we have the second and third matches underneath.

On the second page, is the tournament table with some of the columns removed from the original table on the Wikipedia page. Plus, I've formatted it the way I want.

6 NATIONS RUGBY - TABLE

Pos	Nation	Pld	W	D	L	PF	PA	PD	Points
1	Wales	5	4	0	1	164	103	+61	20
2	France	5	3	0	2	140	103	+37	16
3	Ireland	5	3	0	2	136	88	+48	15
4	Scotland	5	3	0	2	138	91	+47	15
5	England	5	2	0	3	112	121	-9	10
6	Italy	5	0	0	5	55	239	-184	0

OK, let's see how we can produce all of this.

The code

There are 4 script files and 1 HTML file in this project.

1-getData.gs: Gets the data on the RESULTS page and sets them up ready to be added.

2-addResults.gs: This creates the document, sets the styles, gets the country flags, adds the results, and adds some bolding

3-addTable.gs: This gets the data from the TABLE sheet, sets up the styles, adds the data to the table, and deals with some of the formatting from the web page.

4-sendDoc.gs: This emails the document as a PDF and removes the Google Doc from the Drive.

5-email.html: This is the email template.

Script 1
1getData.gs - Get the results data and set it up to be added.

```
1. //Weekly Trigger
2. function getData() {
3.   const ss = SpreadsheetApp.getActiveSpreadsheet(),
4.   shResults = ss.getSheetByName('RESULTS'),
5.   results = shResults.getDataRange().getValues();
```

L2: Open the function.

L3-5: Get the data from the RESULTS sheet.

```
7.          //Get appropriate week data (months 0-11)
8.   const wk1 = new Date(2021, 1, 6),
9.         wk2 = new Date(2021, 1, 13),
10.        wk3 = new Date(2021, 1, 27),
11.        wk4 = new Date(2021, 2, 13),
12.        wk5 = new Date(2021, 2, 20);
```

L8-12: Set up date objects for each of the five weeks of the tournament. These are the Mondays the reports will be sent out on. Note, the months are 0-11, not 1-12, so the above shows 3rd February to 16th March.

```
14.         //Get today's date & dates in array
15.         const todaysDate = new Date().setHours(0, 0, 0, 0);
16.         //const todaysDate = new Date(2021, 1, 13).setHours(0, 0, 0, 0);
        //Test line
17.         const wks = [wk1, wk2, wk3, wk4, wk5];
```

L15: Get today's date at midnight. This will allow us to compare dates correctly.

L16: This is just a test line, as the dates for this tournament have passed, but you can use this line to try the script out. Activate it and comment out line 15.

L17: Add all the Mondays in one array.

```
19.         //Loop thru dates
20.         wks.forEach((wk, w) => {
21.           if (todaysDate === wk.setHours(0, 0, 0, 0)) {
22.           //Get row that matches date
23.           const row = (w * 6);
```

L20: Iterate through the *wks* array.

L21: Check to see if today's date matches one of the Mondays in the array. If so, it'll run the code.

L23: On the sheet, each week's results start every 6 rows, i.e. row 1, 7, 13, etc. So, we convert the array index to the row array number, i.e. 0, 6, 12, etc.

```
25.         //Get data for that game week
26.         const wkInfo = {
27.           homeTeam1: results[row][0]
```

```
28.            .replace("(1 BP)", "").trim(),
29.        awayTeam1: results[row][2]
30.            .replace("(1 BP)", "").trim(),
```

L26: Create an object, *wkInfo*, to store the data.

L27: Create a property called *homeTeam1* and the value will be the first home team. This will be in the first row for that game week and in the first column. In the first week this is "Italy".

France (1 BP)

Italy played France and France received a bonus point. We can see that it is prefixed by (1 BP) as France scored a lot of tries that week, but I don't want that to show it in my document, so we need to remove it from either the home or away team.

L28: We do that by replacing it with an empty value, i.e. "". I also use **trim()** in case there are any empty spaces either side of the country text.

L29-30: We do the same for the away team. The away team's name is in column C.

Now, get the score. On the web page it's presented together, but I want to extract the home team score and the away team score separately.

```
32.        homeScore1: results[row][1].split('-')[0],
33.        awayScore1: results[row][1].split("-")[1],
```

L32: That's easily done. We get the result in the second column and use **split()** and state where we're going to split it. Here, it will be the hyphen. This will produce 2 items in an array (42,0) and we get the first one for the home team score.

L33: We do the same for the away score, but this time get the second item in the array.

So, now our object contains: *homeTeam1: Wales, awayTeam1: Italy, homeScore1: 42* and *awayScore1: 0*.

I also want to get the scorer details.

```
35.        homeScorers1: results[row + 1][0]
36.            .replace(/\*/g, ""),
37.        awayScorers1: results[row + 1][2]
38.            .replace(/\*/g, ""),
```

L35: This is in the row below the country name, so we use *row+1*.

L36: As there was bolding on the original web page, this has been imported with asterisks around the bolded words. I want to get rid of that. So, we use a regular expression, to replace any asterisks with nothing, i.e. remove them.

L37-38: We do the same for the away scorers, getting the third column.

```
40.         homeTeam2: results[row + 2][0]
41.             .replace("(1 BP)", "").trim(),
42.         awayTeam2: results[row + 2][2]
43.             .replace("(1 BP)", "").trim(),
44.
45.         homeScore2: results[row + 2][1].split('-')[0],
46.         awayScore2: results[row + 2][1].split("-")[1],
47.
48.         homeScorers2: results[row + 3][0]
49.             .replace(/\*/g, ""),
50.         awayScorers2: results[row + 3][2]
51.             .replace(/\*/g, ""),
52.
53.         homeTeam3: results[row + 4][0]
54.             .replace("(1 BP)", "").trim(),
55.         awayTeam3: results[row + 4][2]
56.             .replace("(1 BP)", "").trim(),
57.
58.         homeScore3: results[row + 4][1].split('-')[0],
59.         awayScore3: results[row + 4][1].split("-")[1],
60.
61.         homeScorers3: results[row + 5][0]
62.             .replace(/\*/g, ""),
63.         awayScorers3: results[row + 5][2]
64.             .replace(/\*/g, "")
65.     };
```

L40-51: We then repeat the same for the second match. The only difference is that the rows are 2 and 3 lower than the original *row*.

L53-65: Then for the third match, getting the rows that are 5 and 6 lower than *row*. Note, in line 64, we don't add a comma as we're at the end of our object and in line 65 we close the object.

```
67.         const weekNo = w + 1;
68.
69.         //Make and send doc
70.         const docA = addResults(wkInfo, weekNo, ss);
71.         const doc = addTable(ss, docA);
72.         sendDoc(doc, weekNo);
```

```
73.              }
74.          });
75.      }
```

L67: I want to add the week number on the document, so we get the array index *w* and add one.

Now we have the data, we need to make the document.

L70: We call the **addResults()** function which will create the results page. The document will be returned and stored in the variable *docA*.

L71: We call the **addTable()** function which will create the table page. The document will be returned and stored in the variable *doc*.

L72: We call the **sendDoc()** function to email the document as a PDF.

L3-75: We close the if statement, the **forEach()** loop and the function.

Script 2
2-addResults.gs - Add the results to the document.

```
1.  function addResults(wkInfo, weekNo) {
2.    const doc = DocumentApp.create("6 Nations Results");
3.    const body = doc.getBody();
4.
5.    body.setMarginTop(0);
6.    body.setMarginBottom(0);
```

L1: Open the function and pass the *wkInfo* object containing the results data and the week number.

L2-3: Create a new document and get its body.

L5-6: Set the top and bottom margins to 0 to give us a bit more space.

```
8.    //Set styles
9.    const style0 = {};
10.       style0[DocumentApp.Attribute.FONT_FAMILY] = 'Nunito';
11.       style0[DocumentApp.Attribute.FONT_SIZE] = 26;
12.       style0[DocumentApp.Attribute.BOLD] = true;
13.       style0[DocumentApp.Attribute.UNDERLINE] = true;
14.
15.       const style1 = {};
16.       style1[DocumentApp.Attribute.FONT_SIZE] = 22;
17.       style1[DocumentApp.Attribute.BOLD] = true;
```

```
18.        style1[DocumentApp.Attribute.FOREGROUND_COLOR] = '#0000ff';
19.        style1[DocumentApp.Attribute.UNDERLINE] = false;
20.
21.        const style2 = {};
22.        style2[DocumentApp.Attribute.FONT_SIZE] = 14;
23.        style2[DocumentApp.Attribute.BOLD] = false;
24.        style2[DocumentApp.Attribute.FOREGROUND_COLOR] = '#666666';
```

L9-13: We set up the styles and the first one is for the results title.

L15-19: The next is for the teams and scores.

L21-24: This one is for the scorer details.

```
26.        //Add title and results
27.        body.appendParagraph("6 NATIONS RUGBY - WEEK " + weekNo)
28.           .setAttributes(style0);
29.
30.        const ht = [wkInfo.homeTeam1, wkInfo.homeTeam2, wkInfo.homeTeam3];
31.        const at = [wkInfo.awayTeam1, wkInfo.awayTeam2, wkInfo.awayTeam3];
32.        const hs = [wkInfo.homeScore1, wkInfo.homeScore2, wkInfo.homeScore3];
33.        const as = [wkInfo.awayScore1, wkInfo.awayScore2, wkInfo.awayScore3];
34.        const hsr = [wkInfo.homeScorers1, wkInfo.homeScorers2,
      wkInfo.homeScorers3];
35.        const asr = [wkInfo.awayScorers1, wkInfo.awayScorers2,
      wkInfo.awayScorers3];
```

L26-28: Add the title and week number and set the styling.

L30-35: Next, we're going to set up six arrays which will hold the home and away teams for the current week, the home and away scores, and the scorers for the week. Each of these is accessed via its object property we set up in the previous script. We'll use these to then loop through them to add the styling.

```
37.        for (let x = 0; x < 3; x++) {
38.          body.appendParagraph(ht[x] + " " + hs[x]).setAttributes(style1);
39.          body.appendParagraph(hsr[x]).setAttributes(style2);
40.          body.appendParagraph('');
41.          body.appendParagraph(at[x] + " " + as[x]).setAttributes(style1);
42.          body.appendParagraph(asr[x]).setAttributes(style2);
43.          body.appendHorizontalRule();
44.        }
```

L37: Set up a loop to go through the 3 elements in each array.

L38: Append a paragraph with the home team (*ht*) and their score (*hs*) and set the styling.

L39: Append a paragraph with the home team scorers (*hsr*) and set the styling.

L40: Add a blank line.

L41: Append a paragraph with the away team (*at*) and their score (*as*) and set the styling.

L42: Append a paragraph with the home team scorers (*asr*) and set the styling.

L43: Add a horizontal line.

Now, we have the basic data on the page but let's add bolding to some of the words and add the flag images.

```
46.       //Flag icons
47.       const england = DriveApp.getFileById('FILE ID').getBlob();
48.       const france = DriveApp.getFileById('FILE ID').getBlob();
49.       const ireland = DriveApp.getFileById('FILE ID').getBlob();
50.       const italy = DriveApp.getFileById('FILE ID').getBlob();
51.       const scotland = DriveApp.getFileById('FILE ID').getBlob();
52.       const wales = DriveApp.getFileById('FILE ID').getBlob();
```

L47-52: Next, we get the little flag icons that are on our Drive and store the blobs in the respective variables.

```
54.       //Add bolding to Try, Con and Pen and add flag images
55.       const scores = ["Try:", "Con:", "Pen:"];
56.       const flags = [england, france, ireland,
57.       italy, scotland, wales];
58.       const countryNames = ["England", "France", "Ireland",
59.       "Italy", "Scotland", "Wales"];
```

L55: Set up an array for the 3 types of scores (Try, Conversation, or a Penalty) as we're going to bold these.

L56-57: We put our flags in an array.

L58-59: We also put the country names in an array, in the same order as the flags.

```
61.       const countries = [wkInfo.homeTeam1, wkInfo.awayTeam1,
62.       wkInfo.homeTeam2, wkInfo.awayTeam2,
63.       wkInfo.homeTeam3, wkInfo.awayTeam3];
64.
```

```
65.        const iconsInOrder = countries.map((country) => {
66.          return flags[countryNames.indexOf(country)];
67.        });
```

L61-63: We add the country names for that particular week in another array. These are in the order of the matches and what they will look like in the document.

L65: We iterate through the *countries* array.

L66: We then get the index of the country in the array *countryNames* and get the flag that corresponds with that from the *flags* array. We then map that into the *iconsInOrder* array. So, this gets the flags in the order of the countries in the *countries* array.

```
69.        const paragraphs = body.getParagraphs();
70.        for (let p = 3; p < paragraphs.length; p += 3) {
71.          const i = (p / 3) - 1;
72.          paragraphs[p - 1].insertInlineImage(0, iconsInOrder[i])
73.            .setHeight(25).setWidth(25);
74.          const paraScores = paragraphs[p].editAsText();
```

L69: We get the paragraphs in the body.

L70: Then loop through the paragraphs in the body. Note, we move 3 paragraphs at a time, to get the paragraphs that have the country team names (e.g. paragraph 3, 6, etc).

L71: We then need to get the flag index position, which will be a third of the counter *p* minus 1. I.e. It will be flagged in index 0 for paragraph 3 (the first flag).

L72: We then want to insert that image before the team name. We first get the paragraph, insert the image inline, at the child index of 0, using the flag at index *i*.

L73: Set the size of the flag icon.

L74: We then get the paragraph after the image, which contains the scorers' details and get it ready to be edited as text.

```
76.        scores.forEach((score) => {
77.          if (paraScores.findText(score)) {
78.          const scoreText = paraScores.findText(score);
79.          const startScore = scoreText.getStartOffset();
80.          const endScore = scoreText.getEndOffsetInclusive();
81.          paraScores.setBold(startScore, endScore, true);
82.          }
83.        });
```

```
84.            }
```

L76: We loop through the 3 types of scores (Try, Con, and Pen).

L77: As we don't always have all these types of scores, we need to check they exist, so we use **findText()** to look for the text, and if it exists we run the next bit of code.

L78: We then find the text that matches that type of score (e.g. looking for the text "Try:".) It then stores that in *scoreText*.

L79: We then need to find the start and end of that text, as we don't want the whole paragraph. First, we get the start position using **getStartOffset()**.

L80: Then we get the end of the text by using **getEndOffSetInclusive()**.

L81: Finally, we bold that text and pass the start and end positions and state *true* as we want bolding. This will add bolding to the words "Try:", "Con:" and "Pen:" if they are present.

L82-84: We close the if statement, the **forEach** loop and the paragraph **for** loop.

```
85.        body.appendPageBreak();
86.        return doc;
87.      }
```

L85-87: We then add a page break and return the document made so far to script 1, line 70.

Script 3
3-addTable.gs - Add the results table

```
1. function addTable(ss, docA) {
2.    const shTable = ss.getSheetByName('TABLE'),
3.    tableData = shTable.getDataRange().getValues();
```

L1: We open the function and pass the spreadsheet and the document to it.

L2-3: We get the data on the TABLE sheet.

```
5.        //Set up styles
6.        const style3 = {};
7.        style3[DocumentApp.Attribute.FOREGROUND_COLOR] = '#000000';
8.        style3[DocumentApp.Attribute.FONT_SIZE] = 22;
9.        style3[DocumentApp.Attribute.BOLD] = true;
10.
11.        const style4 = {};
12.        style4[DocumentApp.Attribute.FONT_SIZE] = 12;
```

```
13.        style4[DocumentApp.Attribute.BOLD] = false;
```

L6-9: Set up the style for the results title.

L11-13: Set up the style for the table data.

```
15.        const widths = [35, 70, 40, 40, 40, 40, 45, 45, 45, 45];
16.
17.        const body = docA.getBody();
18.        body.appendParagraph("");
19.        body.appendParagraph("6 NATIONS RUGBY - TABLE")
20.            .setAttributes(style3);
```

L15: Set up an array with the table column widths in it to loop through later on.

L17-20: We get the body, add a blank line, add the table title, and style it.

```
22.        const table = body.appendTable();
23.        //Add rows
24.        tableData.forEach((rowData, r) => {
25.          if (r > 0) {
26.            const tableRow = table.appendTableRow();
```

L22: We append the table.

L24: We now need to loop through the table data to create the table rows.

L25: There are two rows with header type information and we only want one for our table. So, we ignore the first header row, and we run this for rows 1 and above.

L26: For each row we first need to append a table row.

```
28.        //Add cells
29.        rowData.forEach((cellInfo, c) => {
30.          if (typeof cellInfo == 'number') {
31.            cellInfo = cellInfo.toFixed(0);
32.          }
```

L29: We then loop through each item in the row to create the columns and cells for each row, i.e. we're moving horizontally across our table row.

L30: As we're going to format any numbers, we first need to check that a number is present. So, we get the type of the variable in that cell and check it's a number.

L31: If it is a number, we set the number format to a whole number, i.e. 0 decimal places, as rugby scores are whole numbers.

```
33.        //Ignore certain columns
34.        if (c < 9 || c > 13) {
35.          //Remove asterisks, set styling & column widths
36.          cellInfo = cellInfo.replace(/\*/g, "");
37.          const cell = tableRow.appendTableCell(cellInfo)
38.                            .setAttributes(style4);
39.          cell.getChild(0).asParagraph()
40.              .setAlignment(DocumentApp.HorizontalAlignment.CENTER);
41.          cell.setWidth(widths[c]);
```

L34: I want to ignore some columns, so we just ignore certain column numbers (or in reality, array position numbers).

L36: I want to get rid of the asterisks like we saw in the results, so again we use a regular expression to first find the asterisks and then with the **replace()** method to get rid of them.

L37-38: Then add the table cell and style it.

L39-40: Add centre horizontal alignment to the cell. Note the need to get the child first.

L41: Finally, we set its width by getting the width from the *width* array.

Now, I want to add a green background and bolding to the header row.

```
43.        //Add header background and bolding
44.        if (r === 1) {
45.          cell.editAsText()
46.              .setBackgroundColor('#93c47d')
47.              .setBold(true);
48.        }
49.        else {
50.          //Add alternative row shading
51.          if (r % 2) {
52.            cell.editAsText()
53.                .setBackgroundColor('#efefef');
54.          }
55.        }
56.      }
57.    });
58.  }
59. });
```

L44: We do this for row 1.

L45-48: Edit the cells as text, set the background colour and bold them.

L49: Now, I want to add the other rows with alternating colours.

L51: First, we check if the row is an even number. If so, we add the background colour, if it's not, we leave it white. We do that by getting the modulo of 2 and if there's no remainder, it returns true.

L52-53: Add a light grey to the cell.

L54-59: Then close the various if-else statements and loops.

```
61.        //Add missing headers and border width
62.        table.getCell(0, 0).setText("Pos");
63.        table.getCell(0, 1).setText("Nation");
64.        table.getCell(0, 9).setText("Points");
65.        table.setBorderWidth(1.2);
66.        docA.saveAndClose();
67.        return docA;
68.      }
```

L62-64: We need to add the header text. We get the specific cells and set the text we want.

L65: Finally, I want the table borders to be a little thicker, so we set the border width to the table.

L66-68: We save and close the document and return the document to script 1, line 71.

Script 4
4-sendDoc.gs - Send the document to the user

```
1. //Email doc to user
2. function sendDoc(doc, weekNo) {
3.   const emailBody = HtmlService.createHtmlOutputFromFile('5-email')
4.                         .getContent();
```

L1: Open the function and pass the document and the week number.

L3-4: We get the HTML from the file "5-email". Note, here we use **createHtmlOutputFromFile()**.

```
6.    //Get G Doc and make a PDF then attach
7.    const pdf = doc.getAs('application/pdf').getBytes();
8.    const attach = {
```

```
9.          fileName: '6 Nations.pdf',
10.         content: pdf,
11.         mimeType: 'application/pdf'
12.         };
```

L7: We convert the document into a PDF.

L8-10: We set the file name, add the content from the variable pdf, and set its mimeType.

```
14.         MailApp.sendEmail("baz@bazroberts.com",
15.         "6 Nations - Week " + weekNo,
16.         '',
17.         {
18.           htmlBody: emailBody,
19.           attachments: [attach]
20.         });
```

L12-16: We then send the email, set the email title, and as we are using HTML, use the option **htmlBody** to add the email content and then add the PDF as an attachment.

```
22.         //Delete Doc from Drive
23.         const document = DriveApp.getFileById(doc.getId());
24.         document.setTrashed(true);
25.       }
```

L19-21: Finally, we delete the document from our Drive.

HTML 1
5-email.html - Email template

```
1. <!DOCTYPE html>
2. <html>
3.
4. <head>
5.   <base target="_top">
6.   <style>
7.     p {
8.       font-family: verdana;
9.       font-size: 1.2em;
10.         }
```

L1-10: We've seen the first few standard lines before. We then set up the styling for the paragraphs.

```
12.          #title {
13.             height: 40px;
14.             padding-top: 10px;
15.             border-left-style: outset;
16.             border-left-color: blue;
17.             border-left-width: 10px;
18.          }
19.       </style>
20.    </head>
```

L12-20: We set up the title styling, which will include a little blue rectangle to the left of the title.

```
22.       <body>
23.         <h2 id="title">6 NATIONS</h2>
24.         <p>Attached are the 6 Nations results and table.</p>
25.         <hr>
26.       </body>
27.
28.    </html>
```

L22-28: We add the title and the main text, followed by a horizontal rule.

On the Monday after the weekend of the matches, the trigger will send the following email:

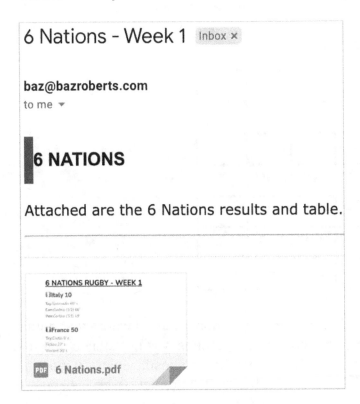

Attached is the PDF it has created with the results and table.

6 NATIONS RUGBY - WEEK 1

Italy 10

Try: Sperandio 65' c
Con: Garbisi (1/1) 66'
Pen: Garbisi (1/1) 19'

France 50

Try: Cretin 6' c
Fickou 27' c
Vincent 30' c
Dulin 49' c
Dupont 53' c
Thomas (2) 57' c, 74' m
Con: Jalibert (6/6) 7', 28', 31', 51', 54', 58'
Pen: Jalibert (1/1) 11'

England 6

Pen: Farrell (2/2) 34', 39'

Scotland 11

Try: Van der Merwe 30' m
Pen: Russell (2/3) 6', 49'

Wales 21

Try: North 49' m
Rees-Zammit 59' c
Con: Halfpenny (1/2) 60'
Pen: Halfpenny (3/3) 5', 19', 66'

Ireland 16

Try: Beirne 37' c
Con: Sexton (1/1) 39'
Pen: Sexton (2/2) 29', 35'

This is the results page for the final week as the championship has now finished.

6 NATIONS RUGBY - TABLE

Pos	Nation	Pld	W	D	L	PF	PA	PD	Points
1	Wales	5	4	0	1	164	103	+61	20
2	France	5	3	0	2	140	103	+37	16
3	Ireland	5	3	0	2	136	88	+48	15
4	Scotland	5	3	0	2	138	91	+47	15
5	England	5	2	0	3	112	121	-9	10
6	Italy	5	0	0	5	55	239	-184	0

Using data from a website can sometimes be a problem as you don't control where that data is on the page. For example, during this tournament one of the matches was postponed due to a Coronavirus outbreak in one of the teams and that meant that match's result wasn't in the table positions it normally would have been. So, I had to update the table index figures on the sheet.

Link to all the file examples and code

Below is a link to a folder with all the example files, which contain all the code seen in this book. You will need to make copies of them to be able to edit them.

Folder containing examples of all the files:
https://bit.ly/GAS4BazRoberts

Final note from the author

As you hopefully can see, once you get your head around how the Document Service works and is structured, it's relatively easy to create a wide-range of documents.

I also hope that along the way you have learnt more about how the different apps work together and can also see that we can go beyond those apps, creating our own web apps and connect to data stored in web pages.

If you have any questions about the content of this book, then please contact me at baz@bazroberts.com

This book is the fourth one in a series on Google Apps Script. If you haven't already, I would also recommend reading the previous ones, which cover working with Google Sheets, Google Forms, and Google Drive.

To give you further practice, I have two books full of practical examples - Projects 1 and 2.

Finally, if you need extra help with JavaScript and want to see more examples of using it in Apps Script, I also have a JavaScript Fundamentals book.

Beginner's Guide to Google Apps Script 1 - Sheets	Beginner's Guide to Google Apps Script 2 - Forms	Beginner's Guide to Google Apps Script 3 - Drive	Step-by-step Guide to Google Apps Script 4 - Documents

Google Apps Script Projects 1	Google Apps Script Projects 2	JavaScript Fundamentals for Apps Script Users
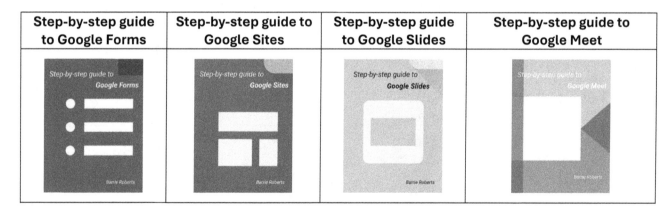		

Finally, I big thank you for buying this book. I really do hope it's helped you with writing some great code.

Barrie "Baz" Roberts – Rev 10

Other books and ebooks available by this author on Amazon:

Beginner's Guide to Google Drive	Beginner's Guide to Google Sheets	Beginner's Guide to Google Docs	Google Sheet Functions – A step-by-step guide

Step-by-step guide to Google Forms	Step-by-step guide to Google Sites	Step-by-step guide to Google Slides	Step-by-step guide to Google Meet

I also post and share blog posts and information related to Google Apps Script and Google Workspace on my website www.bazroberts.com and on LinkedIn: www.linkedin.com/in/bazroberts/